D1530958

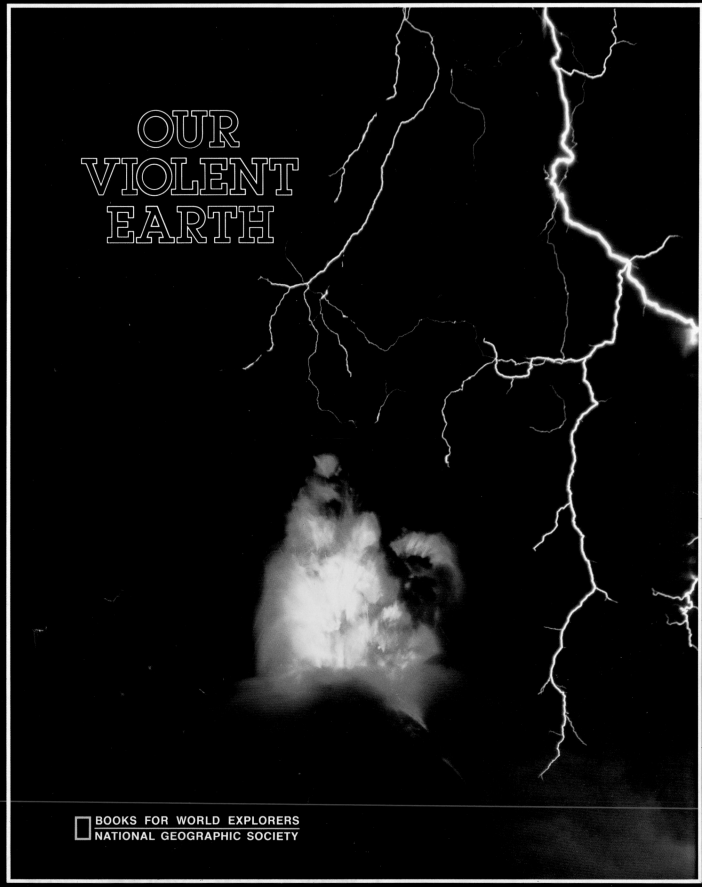

OUR VIOLENT EARTH

BOOKS FOR WORLD EXPLORERS
NATIONAL GEOGRAPHIC SOCIETY

CONTENTS

TITLE PAGE: *Earth and atmosphere stage a light show above Volcán de Fuego, "Volcano of Fire," in Guatemala, in Central America.*
TITLE PAGE: BYRON CRADER/TOM STACK & ASSOCIATES

COVER: *A river of red-hot lava flows down the slopes of Kilauea, a volcano in Hawaii. The lava will cool and harden.*
COVER: ROBIN T. HOLCOMB/U. S. GEOLOGICAL SURVEY

What a mess! Employees of a California supermarket put fallen coffee cans back on a shelf after an earthquake in the San Fernando Valley. This 1971 quake did more than tip cans from shelves. The shock waves toppled buildings, damaged freeways, and buckled train tracks.

NATIONAL GEOGRAPHIC PHOTOGRAPHER JAMES P. BLAIR

GIANFRANCO GORGONI/CONTACT

EARTHQUAKES

Citizens of Gemona, Italy, wander through their shattered city. On the night of May 6, 1976, a strong earthquake jolted Europe. The most severe damage occurred in northeastern Italy, where about a thousand people died and many more were left homeless.

Earthquakes are caused by movement of the rock that makes up the earth's crust, or outer layer. Millions of earthquakes occur every year. Most are so faint they can be detected only with sensitive equipment. About 700 quakes each year cause damage.

3

VOLCANOES

From a safe distance, Indians watch as Mount St. Helens shoots smoke and burning ash into the night sky. Off and on during the mid-1800s, the volcano released steam, ash, and red-hot lava. Then it lay quiet for more than a hundred years — not erupting again until May 1980. Artist Paul Kane made this painting of Mount St. Helens in 1847. He painted it from Indian descriptions of an eruption that had taken place a few years earlier. Indians who lived near the volcano believed that the mountain was home to a tribe of savages. They refused to go with Kane when he went close to the mountain to explore it.

"We had just come home from church when we saw weird clouds filling the sky," says Melissa Miller, 10, of Ephrata, Washington (left). "A neighbor told us they were ash clouds from Mount St. Helens, which had just erupted." Here Melissa watches the blackening sky with her mother and her grandmother. Layers of ash from the 1980 blast fell on portions of 11 states.
DOUGLAS MILLER

DAVID FALCONER

Six months after Mount St. Helens sent mudflows spilling down river valleys, dried mud still half-fills a house in Castle Rock, Washington (above). From inside, Michael Sturgill, a resident of Castle Rock, and one of his neighbors, David Turner, 12, peer out a window. The house belongs to another neighbor. The teacher and David are helping the neighbor by digging out mud and searching for belongings buried in it. The house itself was a total loss.

STORMY WEATHER

Spinning down from dark storm clouds, a tornado flattened this girl's house in Wichita Falls, Texas (right). At any given time, about 2,000 storms are occurring on earth. Some storms benefit the earth by carrying heat and water to places where they are needed. But stormy weather can be dangerous. Tornadoes, hurricanes, and lightning are some of the mightiest forces on earth. Every year violent storms rage through areas where people live. Now satellites and special instruments help in forecasting the weather. Scientists can warn threatened communities of approaching storms and thus help save lives.

BREWER & LAFFERTY/BLACK STAR

DROUGHT AND FIRE

KERBY SMITH

On a Texas farm, a man picks up a handful of soil that drought has turned to dust (left). A fire fighter in New Mexico battles a blaze with shovelfuls of soil (right). Though both men wish for rain, neither can count on a downpour when he needs it. Most places on earth have experienced either drought or fire at some time. But people are finding ways to deal with these natural disasters when they strike.

6

JAMES A. SUGAR/WOODFIN CAMP, INC.

CALIFORNIA: FIRE AND RAIN

When floodwaters threaten a town, the citizens turn out to try to save it. Here a teenager in Malibu, California, stacks sandbags against a wooden fence in an attempt to hold back a coming flood. Residents hope the sandbag barrier will prevent houses behind the fence from being washed away. Months earlier, fire destroyed much of the plant life on nearby hills. Now heavy downpours have washed mud and brush from the slopes. The rain has cut deep gullies between remaining patches of green brush. In southern California, fire and rain join forces to strip hillsides of trees, brush, grass, and soil. The result: floods and mud slides.

WATER

Carrying his goods to safety, a merchant wades along a flooded walkway in Venice. An Italian city built on a group of islands, Venice has been sinking into the sea for years. Many people fear that the continuous wearing action of seawater will someday destroy the city's centuries-old buildings.

Water is one of earth's most powerful forces. Over millions of years, water in the form of rain wears away mountains. Glaciers, mighty rivers of ice, slowly mow down forests and scoop out the basins that will later hold lakes. Water contributes to erosion that scars parts of the land. Masses of tumbling snow called avalanches race down mountain slopes, crushing houses and overturning trains. In its gentler moods, water is a friend, essential to life. Fortunately, people are learning more and more about ways of dealing with water when it is not so gentle.

1
EARTHQUAKES

by Catherine O'Neill

Villagers in Peru pick their way through streets filled with crumbled buildings. An earthquake jolted this South American country in May 1970. Here, in Huarás, it left standing only the skeletons of a few structures. The quake set off a huge avalanche of mud and ice from Peru's highest mountain peak. Roaring down at 200 miles (322 km)* an hour, the avalanche swept away entire villages. When the quake and avalanche were over, 50,000 people had been killed and 800,000 had been left homeless. The Peruvian earthquake was one of the most violent natural disasters ever recorded in the Western Hemisphere.

FRED WARD/BLACK STAR

* Metric figures in this book are given in rounded numbers.

8

When the Land Trembles

The earth under our feet usually feels firm. But during an earthquake it trembles. It may sway and roll, bending railroad tracks like ribbons. The motion can send mountainsides plunging into valleys.

Earthquakes happen when forces deep within our planet cause movement of the earth's outer layer, called the crust. When pieces of the crust move, they sometimes release energy in the form of shock waves. We feel the waves as the tremors, or shaking, of earthquakes.

When a large earthquake occurs at a place where many people live, it can cause tremendous destruction. Scientists today are working on ways to predict quakes. They hope to be able to save lives and property.

White scars and hanging clouds of dust mark places where landslides carried away earth and rock from the sides of mountains. An earthquake triggered the slides. It hit Guatemala in February 1976 when part of the earth's crust shifted. The quake caused 23,000 deaths in this Central American country.

N.G.S. PHOTOGRAPHER ROBERT W. MADDEN

Carrying groceries, a Guatemalan woman steps from a store jolted by an earthquake (left). This quake damaged more than 300 adobe villages. Adobe—sun-dried clay and straw—crumbles easily. After the quake, the government urged people to build with stronger materials.

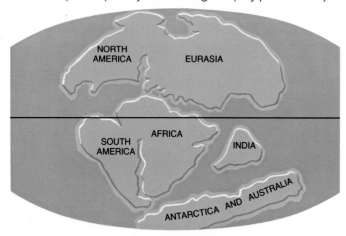

Geologists believe that 225 million years ago all the landmasses had drifted together, forming one huge continent (above). They call it Pangaea (say pan-GEE-uh).

Drifting Continents

Geologists are scientists who study the earth and its makeup. They believe that the earth's crust covers a deep layer of extremely hot rock called the mantle. The heat, they say, creates very slow moving currents in the mantle.

The crust also is rock. It is divided into large plates, or slabs, 10 to 60 miles (16–97 km) thick. The currents in the mantle move these plates slowly around the globe. The plates carry continents and ocean floors with them as they move. But the plates are drifting so slowly that we have no sense of the motion. North America and Europe are moving apart at a rate of about one inch (2½ cm) a year.

Geologists call this movement plate tectonics. Over ages, plate tectonics has changed the look of our planet. Study the maps on this page to see that change—and to see how earth may look far in the future.

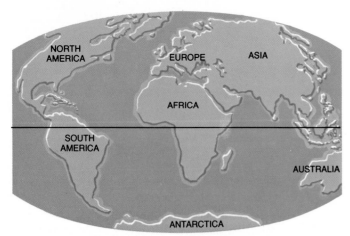

By 160 million years ago, the supercontinent had largely broken up. A sea, the ancestor of the Mediterranean, had formed between Africa and Eurasia.

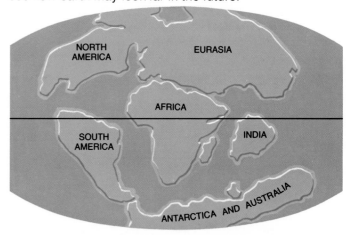

By 65 million years ago, Africa and South America were moving apart. The Atlantic and Indian Oceans had become larger. India was drifting toward Eurasia.

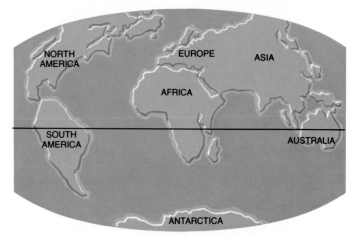

Today the continents have these familiar outlines. Scientists believe the face of the earth will continue to change as landmasses keep drifting.

In 50 million years, our planet may change greatly. The Mediterranean Sea, for example, may become a salty lake. Part of California may split off as an island.

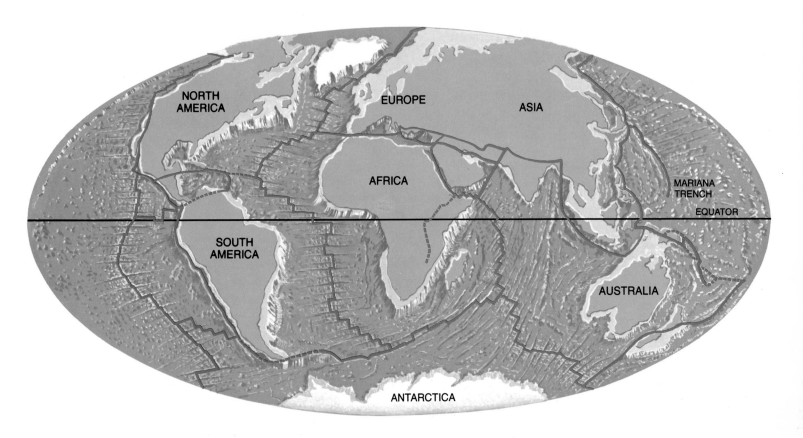

Earth's Moving Plates

The rock plates that make up the earth's crust number about 20. You can see the boundaries of major plates marked in red on the map above. Most earthquakes occur along these boundaries. As the mantle moves plates slowly around the globe, the plates may scrape against each other. Sometimes the pressure along the edges becomes so great that something has to give way. Bent to the breaking point, a plate edge shifts suddenly. Then the land trembles with an earthquake.

Where plates ram into each other head-on, rock near the boundary can be forced up to form mountains. Geologists believe the Himalayas—the highest mountains in the world—were formed when the plate carrying India bumped into the one carrying the rest of Asia.

The deepest place on earth is the Mariana Trench, under the Pacific Ocean. Its floor lies nearly 7 miles (11 km) below sea level. The trench formed when two plates collided and one plunged under the other.

The mantle may also pull plates apart. That's what is causing North America to drift ever farther away from Europe. Scientists believe East Africa is breaking away from the rest of the African continent. In millions of years it may be a new continent, separated from Africa by a new ocean.

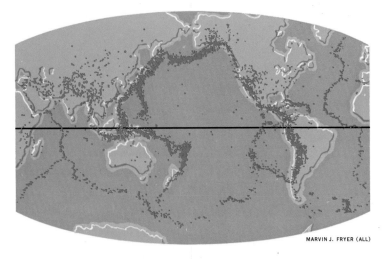

MARVIN J. FRYER (ALL)

Dots on the map above show where earthquakes have occurred. Most earthquakes happen along boundaries between crustal plates. These are the thick slabs of rock that make up the earth's crust. At the boundaries, the plates sometimes grind against each other. The grinding sets up strain that can result in earthquakes. Since most plate boundaries are on the ocean floor, most earthquakes actually occur under the ocean. More than half of all earthquakes occur at the edge of the Pacific plate—the Ring of Fire. You'll read about the violent effects of some ocean quakes on page 19.

San Andreas Fault

It happened at daybreak on April 18, 1906. Along the San Andreas Fault, a plate boundary that runs through California, the ground shuddered. In San Francisco, just east of the fault, the ground shook for 45 seconds. Streets buckled. Buildings collapsed. Toppling wood stoves and kerosene lamps started raging fires that swept through city block after city block. Finally, three days later, the fires were brought under control. By that time, 28,000 buildings had been destroyed and tens of thousands of people had been left homeless. The earthquake had all but demolished San Francisco. Miraculously, fewer than 500 people had died.

San Francisco's citizens quickly set about rebuilding their city. Within ten years, few traces of the disaster were left. But the threat of more quakes remains. Geologists estimate that the crustal plates that meet along the San Andreas Fault may have *(Continued on page 17)*

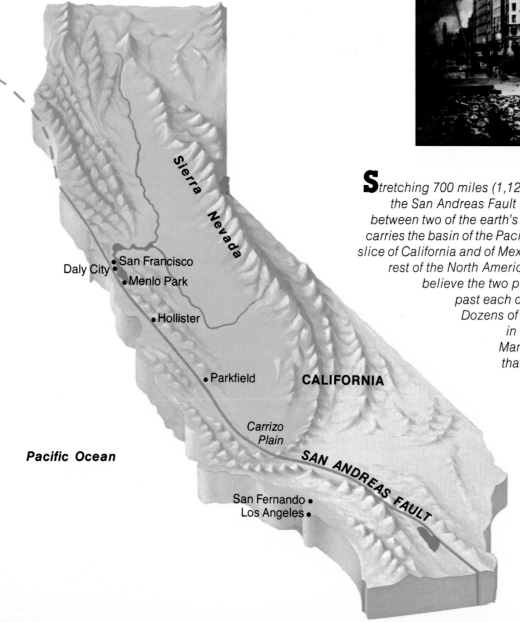

Stretching 700 miles (1,127 km) through California, the San Andreas Fault (left) marks the boundary between two of the earth's crustal plates. One plate carries the basin of the Pacific Ocean and includes a slice of California and of Mexico. The other carries the rest of the North American continent. Geologists believe the two plates have been grinding past each other for millions of years. Dozens of small earthquakes occur in the fault zone every year. Many scientists think it likely that a large quake will strike along the fault before the end of this century.

MARK SEIDLER, N.G.S.

Smoke pours from buildings along San Francisco's Market Street after the 1906 earthquake (above). Movement along the San Andreas Fault caused the disaster. Here National Guardsmen patrol the street to prevent looting.

Earthquake-resistant Transamerica Pyramid pierces the San Francisco skyline. In the foreground stands an older building that could prove to be a hazard during a quake. One danger: the overhanging edge of the roof could crack off, injuring pedestrians below. New buildings must be designed for safety during an earthquake. Engineers expect that if a quake hits, the Transamerica Pyramid will sway with the tremors and thus avoid damage.

(*Continued from page 14*)   been scraping past each other for 100 million years. Sometimes the movement causes earthquakes. But the movement itself usually is so slow—about one inch (2½ cm) a year—that people cannot see it or feel it.

The western side of the fault, the Pacific plate, moves in a northerly direction. It grinds against the North American plate. Over time, the steady movement has shaped part of California's landscape. In the Carrizo Plain, 100 miles (161 km) north of Los Angeles, the fault has left a jagged scar in the earth (left). In some places, it has pushed aside streams and displaced high mountains and rolling hills.

Earthquakes continue to occur along the fault. People hope that if another major quake hits, modern buildings and safety procedures will prevent a tragedy. Meanwhile, scientists are trying to learn how to predict earthquakes. You'll read about some of their studies on pages 18–21.

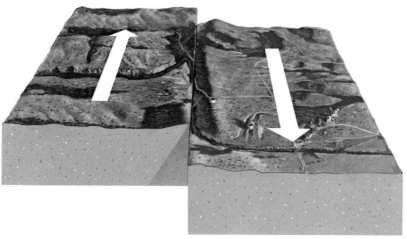

Leaving a scar on the earth's surface, the San Andreas Fault cuts across California's Carrizo Plain (left). The fault penetrates the earth's crust to a depth of at least 20 miles (32 km). Jagged hills mark the boundary between two great crustal plates. The diagram above shows how the plates grind against each other. The Pacific plate, at right, moves northward past the North American plate.

Slow movement along the San Andreas Fault has cracked this concrete drainage ditch at a vineyard near Hollister, California (above). Here vineyard manager Peter Becker measures the crack. It's about 8 inches (20 cm) wide.

Houses in Daly City face two kinds of landslide threats. The city lies along the San Andreas Fault—and beside the Pacific Ocean. Earthquakes and the wearing action of ocean waves and spray result in landslides like the one that occurred here. Laws now prohibit builders from constructing houses in hazardous areas.

Cleaning up after a 1971 earthquake that rattled his home in San Fernando, California, a boy rolls up a fallen window shade. The quake hit at 6 a.m. It lasted ten seconds and damaged a thousand buildings.

SAFETY TIPS

- It's natural to be frightened during an earthquake, but try not to panic. Keep cool!

- If you are indoors, take cover under a bed or under a sturdy table or desk. The furniture will help protect you from falling objects and from flying glass.

- If you are outdoors, look for the nearest open space away from buildings and head for that. Lie flat on the ground.

- After the quake, wear shoes both indoors and out to protect against broken glass.

Earthquake Prediction

Can cockroaches tell when an earthquake is coming? Some scientists think so. In California, researchers studied roaches, using sensitive equipment designed to record movement. It turned out that the roaches were unusually active just before earthquakes.

Someday the results of experiments such as this one may help scientists predict earthquakes accurately. Throughout China, people watch insects and other animals, and report unusual behavior to scientists. In 1975, Chinese scientists observing animal behavior and other signs predicted that an earthquake would soon hit. Officials evacuated 100,000 people from the northeastern city of Haicheng. A few hours later, a large quake leveled the city. Unfortunately, such accurate predictions are still rare. Only a year later, a major earthquake struck east central China without warning. It killed 700,000 people in the city of Tangshan alone.

Often the side effects of an earthquake do more damage than the tremors themselves. Earthquakes often trigger fires. They can send huge ocean waves crashing into coastlines. They *(Continued on page 20)*

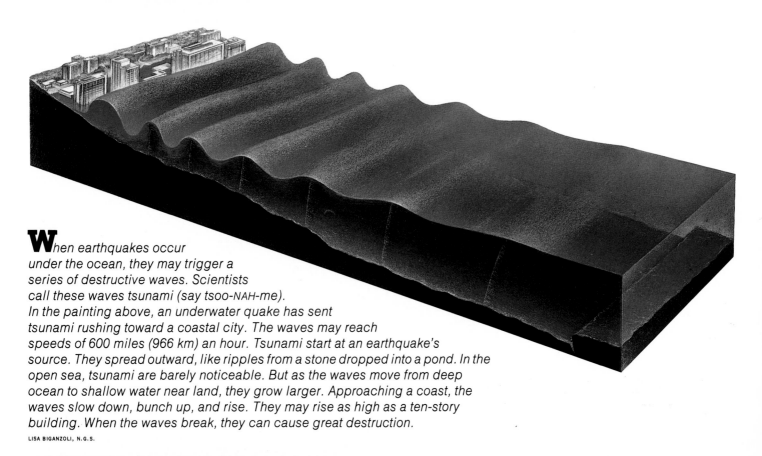

When earthquakes occur
under the ocean, they may trigger a
series of destructive waves. Scientists
call these waves tsunami (say tsoo-NAH-me).
In the painting above, an underwater quake has sent
tsunami rushing toward a coastal city. The waves may reach
speeds of 600 miles (966 km) an hour. Tsunami start at an earthquake's
source. They spread outward, like ripples from a stone dropped into a pond. In the
open sea, tsunami are barely noticeable. But as the waves move from deep
ocean to shallow water near land, they grow larger. Approaching a coast, the
waves slow down, bunch up, and rise. They may rise as high as a ten-story
building. When the waves break, they can cause great destruction.

LISA BIGANZOLI, N.G.S.

Sweeping locomotives and boxcars from
railroad tracks, a huge wave 30 feet (9 m) high
speeds into Seward, Alaska. Oil that spilled
from a storage tank burns on top of the wave. This
was the second of several tsunami to slam into
the town. The 1964 Alaska earthquake that
started it also sent tsunami speeding toward
California, Hawaii, Chile, and Japan. The quake
was the largest ever recorded in North America.
Today the National Weather Service runs the
Tsunami Warning Center, in Honolulu, Hawaii.
Scientists there keep a round-the-clock watch.
They warn people in 14 nations in and around
the Pacific Ocean if tsunami threaten. Then
people can move from coastal areas to higher
ground. Some tsunami travel at the speed of a jet
plane, so early warnings are vital.

PIERRE MION

19

To see if there has been movement along a fault, scientists at a laboratory in Hollister, California, flash a laser—a strong beam of light—3 miles (5 km) across a valley. It bounces off a reflector on the other side of the fault. Instruments measure the travel time of the laser from its source to the reflector and back. If the land has moved along the fault since the last measurement, the travel time of the beam will change. Using this method, scientists make accurate measurements of movements in the earth's crust. Someday this may help them predict earthquakes.

CHARLES O'REAR/WEST LIGHT (ALL)

(Continued from page 18) can slosh lake water out of its basin, causing a flood. Reliable earthquake prediction could help people avoid dangers such as these.

In areas where earthquakes are likely to occur, geologists use sensitive instruments to gather information. These instruments measure the slow creeping of crustal plates. They record even the slightest tremors. By analyzing the information the instruments give them—and by such other means as studying animal behavior—scientists move closer to making reliable earthquake prediction a reality. Someday they may be able to alert people: "Warning! Earthquake expected tomorrow!"

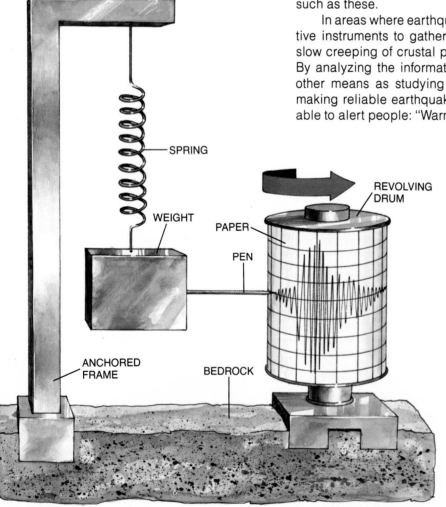

SPRING

WEIGHT

REVOLVING DRUM

PAPER

PEN

ANCHORED FRAME

BEDROCK

To record earthquakes, scientists use an instrument called a seismograph (say SIZE-muh-graf). A frame and a revolving drum are anchored in bedrock, solid rock under the soil. A weight is suspended from the frame by a spring. A pen attached to the weight traces a line on paper wrapped around the drum. The line is called a seismogram. Usually the line is straight. But during a quake the weight stays in place while the drum moves up and down. That makes the line wavy. Scientists estimate the magnitude, or strength, of a quake by measuring the waves. They describe the magnitude of earthquakes in a series of numbers called the Richter scale. Each number stands for a quake that releases 30 times more energy than a quake of the next lower number. For example, an earthquake of magnitude 7 sets loose 30 times more energy than one of magnitude 6.

BARBARA GIBSON

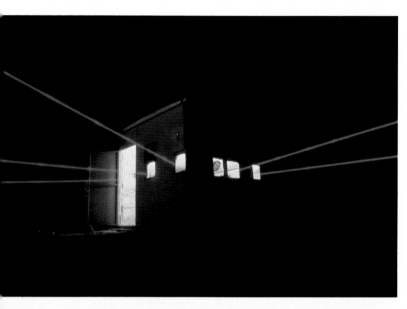

Laser beams streak from an observatory in Hollister, California. Each one speeds toward a reflector like the one shown on page 20. From this study, geologists have learned that the land along a nearby fault is moving. They have also learned that the land does not always move at the same pace. It speeds up and slows down.

At the U. S. Geological Survey laboratory in Menlo Park, California (below), Wesley Hall reads a seismogram. Hall heads a project that maintains seismographs at 400 sites throughout California and Oregon. This wavy seismogram tells him that a small quake has occurred near the town of Parkfield. Studying information obtained at the sites, geologists seek hints of future earthquakes.

2
VOLCANOES

by Catherine O'Neill

River of mud spills down the Toutle River valley, in Washington, on the day Mount St. Helens erupted in 1980. Hot ash and rock from the blast melted snow and ice on the slopes. The meltwater combined with the ash and with loosened earth to form huge masses of mud. The blast blew the top off the mountain, once a popular spot for hiking and camping. When volcanoes erupt, they often create spectacular fireworks as they spit out red-hot ash and lava. Eruptions may also trigger fires, floods, and avalanches. Volcanoes form when heat and pressure force melted rock upward from deep inside the earth. The melted rock bursts through cracks in the earth's surface as lava or ash.

TOM ZIMBEROFF/SYGMA

Mount St. Helens

Until a sunny Sunday morning in May 1980, Mount St. Helens was a splendid sight. Its snowcapped peak jutted from surrounding green forests. A crystal lake sparkled at its base. Backpackers liked to explore the peak, which lies in the Cascade Range in Washington State. Every year, the mountain's beauty attracted thousands of vacationers. Although its cone shape reminded visitors of its volcanic history, Mount St. Helens had not erupted for more than a hundred years.

But in the early spring of 1980, the volcano began to awaken. During March, scientists recorded dozens of earthquakes originating under the mountain. Near the end of March, the peak began spitting out small amounts of steam and ash. A bulge appeared on the mountain's north slope. By mid-April, the bulge had swelled to 300 feet (91 m) thick. It was like a huge blister ready to pop. Scientists could tell that something big was about to happen to Mount St. Helens.

State officials evacuated a 20-mile-wide (32-km) danger zone around the mountain. The only people they allowed in were those with good reason for being there. Such people included loggers, as well as

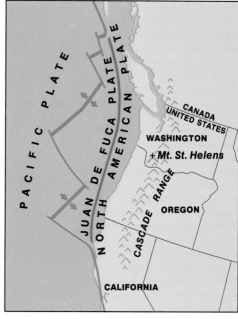

PETER J. BALCH, N.G.S.

Geologists believe the Cascade Range (above), which includes Mount St. Helens, has been forming for millions of years. It lies near the boundary of two crustal plates (green line). The Juan de Fuca plate is moving eastward and plunging under the North American plate. On page 35, you'll see how this movement builds mountains.

Great clouds of gas, ash, and steam gush from Mount St. Helens (left). A huge blast tore away the mountain's northern face on the morning of May 18, 1980. The volcano had been dormant, or inactive, for 123 years.

ROGER WERTH/WOODFIN CAMP & ASSOCIATES

Before the blast, snowcapped Mount St. Helens and the forests surrounding it had a picture-postcard beauty (above, left). Every year, thousands of visitors explored the area.

TOM AND PAT LEESON

After the eruption, the area around Mount St. Helens was gray and lifeless. The blast tore away a portion of the peak equal in height to the Empire State Building. It killed more than two million animals.

N.G.S. PHOTOGRAPHER JAMES P. BLAIR

scientists and photographers who wanted to record the coming events.

Those events started on May 18 at 8:32 in the morning. A message came over shortwave radios. It was from a young geologist 6 miles (10 km) away from the mountain. *"Vancouver! Vancouver! This is it . . . ,"* the message said. Moments later the scientist was dead, killed by a huge explosion that had ripped through the northern face of the peak. By the time the eruption ended, about 60 other people were dead. A blanket of gray ash covered the land for miles around. A large area stretching north from Mount St. Helens was changed from a scenic vacation spot to a landscape as barren as the moon's.

Seconds before the eruption, a huge avalanche roared down the north slope. Then gases from deep inside the volcano burst from the peak. Masses of rock and hot

Once this fir tree towered above the forest floor (below). Now all that stands is a stump bristling with splinters. Foresters Byron Rickert, left, and Mike Bickford inspect the damage. This tree may have grown for 300 years. The volcano's fury destroyed it in seconds.

HARLEY SOLTES/EUGENE REGISTER-GUARD

Cut down by the eruption, fallen evergreens look like scattered matchsticks (above). Many of these trees had grown as tall as a 15-story building. But all living plants in the area, from the tallest tree to the smallest shrub, died with the first blast. Hurricane-force winds carrying ash, rock, and mud knocked down every object in their path. The winds mowed down millions of trees across 200 square miles (518 sq km) of timberland. Luckily, the eruption occurred on a Sunday. On a weekday, hundreds of loggers would have been at work among the evergreens.

JAMES A. SUGAR

ash gushed from the crater, melting ice and snow on the slopes. The meltwater combined with ash and earth to form a huge river of mud. It raced down the mountain into river valleys below, destroying all bridges, roads, and houses in its path. A great column of steam and ash shot 12 miles (19 km) into the sky. Blown eastward, clouds of ash blackened the sky for more than 250 miles (402 km). The explosion was so loud that people 225 miles to the north heard it. The energy it released was 500 times greater than that released by the atomic bomb dropped on Hiroshima, in Japan, during World War II.

Extremely hot winds blew with hurricane force. They toppled trees in a fan-shaped area up to 18 miles (29 km) from the blast. Later, officials inspected the area from a helicopter. They said the slopes around the volcano looked as if they were covered with matchsticks.

When the clouds of ash around the volcano cleared, observers

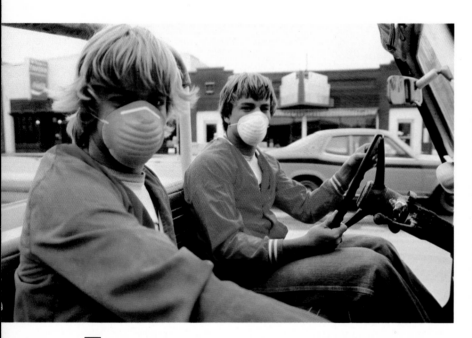

Face masks protect two teenagers in Yakima from volcanic ash. A blanket of the fine powder fell on the city, 85 miles (137 km) from the blast site. Winds carried the ash. People in Yakima and elsewhere in Washington used masks, bandannas, and even paper coffee filters to keep the ash out of their lungs.

JAMES MASON/BLACK STAR (BOTH)

Gray volcanic ash dusts a red rose in Portland, Oregon—a city famous for its rose gardens. The gardens were in full bloom at the time of the ashfall.

Darkness falls in the morning as an ash cloud blackens the sky over southwestern Washington. The volcanic cloud blocked out the sun, causing the streetlight, at right, to come on. Such lights are set to turn on automatically in the evening darkness. This ash comes from an eruption that occurred a week after the big blast. Here a passing car has stirred up fallen ash along a highway.

L. JOSEPH NEIBAUER/NATURAL GRAPHICS

could see that the top of the mountain was gone. Before the eruption, Mount St. Helens had a pointed peak. Now the summit was a horseshoe-shaped crater that measured more than a mile (1½ km) wide. Vents, or cracks, in the crater floor released steam and gas. Later, lava formed a dome that eventually grew several hundred feet high.

Violent though it was, the blast was small compared with some earlier eruptions in other parts of the world. In 1815, a volcano called Tambora, in Indonesia, spit out 80 times as much ash and other material as Mount St. Helens did! Geologists believe Mount St. Helens will not explode again for many years the way it did on May 18, 1980. But small eruptions of ash, steam, and lava may continue for years to come.

Today about 600 active volcanoes dot the earth. More than half of them are on the Ring of Fire, the rim of the Pacific Ocean basin where earthquakes frequently occur (see the map on page 13). Scientists say volcanic eruptions have been occurring for hundreds of millions of years. You'll find out what causes them on pages 34–35.

Logjam carried by the mudflow bulldozes a bridge that had spanned the Toutle River (above). The bridge snapped just moments before this picture was made. The mudflow raged through the Toutle River valley, below the volcano. It forced 2,000 people to flee their homes.

ROGER WERTH/WOODFIN CAMP & ASSOCIATES

Surrounded by mud, two youngsters play a game on the top of a pickup truck in Toutle, Washington (right). Tom Harper, left, and Amy Halleck, both 10, salvaged the game from Amy's house, in the background. The eruption sent a mudflow crashing into the house. The game was one of the few things left untouched.

RALPH PERRY

30

Nearly a year after the eruption, geologist John Dvorak explores the crater that the blast left behind (above). Steam escaping from underground has condensed, forming the cloud of vapor that surrounds him. Behind Dvorak is the rounded top of a lava dome. The dome formed from lava flowing through cracks, called vents, in the crater floor. The lava cooled, hardening into a dome.

JAMES A. SUGAR

Adam Bay, 13, of Silver Lake, Washington, listens to a radio for news of Mount St. Helens (right). Adam and his family live only 100 feet (30 m) from the red zone, the restricted area around the volcano. People in Adam's neighborhood keep themselves informed by radio in case eruption threatens again. As Adam listens, he does his homework. What subject is he studying? Volcanoes!

DAVID FALCONER (ABOVE AND OPPOSITE)

Geologists measure movement on the crater floor (below). Melted rock called magma is rising from far below, creating a bulge in the floor. Christina Heliker, left, and Don Swanson measure the swelling bulge with a surveying telescope called a theodolite (say thee-ODD-uh-lite). With this instrument, geologists take measurements that tell them how much the bulge has grown. Although Mount St. Helens is still active, geologists think that another huge blast is unlikely to occur for a long time. But smaller eruptions may continue for years to come.

RALPH PERRY

In a physical-science class at Toutle Lake Junior High, students work with lab samples found in their own backyards (left). Teacher John Brugman and his seventh-grade class examine a lump of lava called a bomb. Bombs form when masses of molten lava thrown from an erupting volcano cool and harden before hitting the ground. This bomb consists of volcanic rock called pumice (say PUM-iss). In powdered form, pumice is used as a gritty cleanser. Dentists sometimes polish teeth with it.

Red-hot lava flows in a surface crack just a few feet from geologist Maurice Sako's boots (above). Sako is studying Mauna Ulu volcano, in Hawaii. "Mauna Ulu" means "Growing Mountain" in the Hawaiian language. The volcano poured out lava from 1969 through 1974. Here the surface of a lava stream has cooled and hardened into a rock crust. Beneath it, molten lava continues to flow. All Hawaiian volcanoes are called hot-spot volcanoes.

ROBIN T. HOLCOMB/U. S. GEOLOGICAL SURVEY

Curtains of fiery lava rise behind the town of Vestmannaeyjar, in Iceland (above). In 1973, lava suddenly began erupting from a vent in the earth. Some homes stood only about a thousand feet (305 m) from the lava fountains. Ash buried many houses. Lava burned and crushed others. Luckily, all the residents escaped. Weeks later, however, a man entering his cellar died from poisonous volcanic gases that had been trapped there. Scientists named the new volcano Eldfell, "Fire Mountain." Eldfell, like Iceland's other volcanoes, is of the rift type. That is, it formed along a rift, or crack, in the earth's crust.

SIGURDUR THORARINSSON

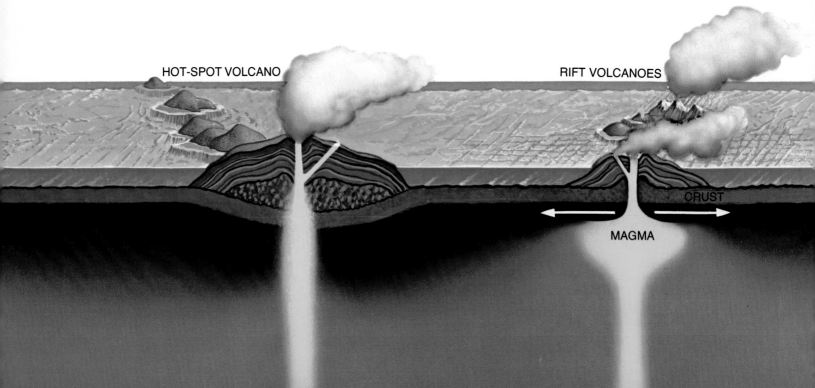

HOT-SPOT VOLCANO

RIFT VOLCANOES

CRUST

MAGMA

How Volcanoes Form

Beneath the earth's crust lies a hot, deep layer of rock called the mantle. Some of the mantle is molten, or melted. It forms a hot, flowing substance called magma. Extreme pressure forces magma through weak spots in the earth's crust. Where the magma breaks through the crust, volcanoes form. The magma that erupts at the surface is called lava.

Some volcanoes are born at places where the huge, shifting plates that form the earth's crust bump into each other and one plate sinks beneath another. These are called subduction volcanoes. Others, called rift volcanoes, form in places where plates move apart. Still others — hot-spot volcanoes — are created where rising magma melts holes through crustal plates.

Some volcanoes send out mostly lava; others spit out rock, ash, and gas as well. Volcanoes are like windows in the earth's crust. They reveal a lot about what is happening beneath the surface of the earth.

Volcanoes form in three basic ways. Hot-spot volcanoes appear where magma from the mantle melts holes in the crust and rises to the surface (below, left). Rift volcanoes form where crustal plates split apart. As the plates separate (below, center), magma rises from the rift. Subduction volcanoes occur where plates collide (below, right). One plate may slip underneath another, causing surface rock on the lower plate to melt. Then the magma rises through weak spots in the overlying plate.

Eruptions of Mount St. Helens and of other volcanoes in the Cascades tell geologists that the range is still forming. Two crustal plates are colliding, producing the magma that builds the mountains. The collision has been happening for millions of years and may continue for millions more. Volcanoes formed from such a collision are called subduction volcanoes.

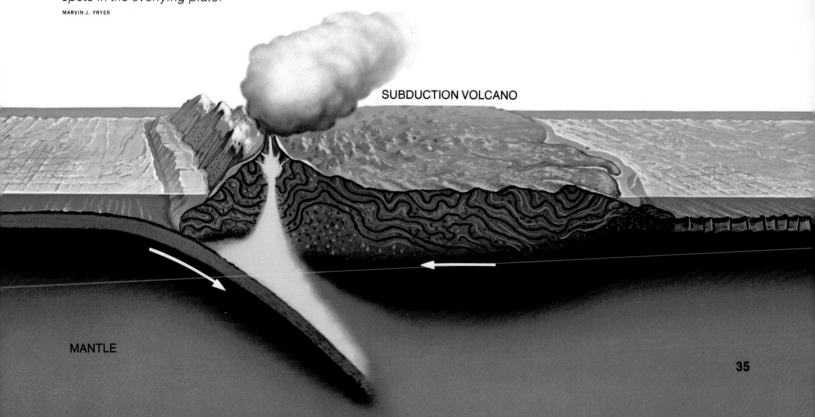

SUBDUCTION VOLCANO

MANTLE

Fiery Iceland

The island country of Iceland lies near the Arctic Circle in the chill waters of the North Atlantic Ocean. Yet on November 14, 1963, waters off the island's southern coast began to boil!

A volcano erupting on the ocean floor had heated the water to the boiling point. The following night, a narrow ridge of land appeared through the waves. An island was born. A year and a half later, the new island measured nearly one mile (1$\frac{1}{2}$ km) wide. Icelanders named it Surtsey, after the Norse god of fire.

Surtsey is just one example of the frequent volcanic activity in Iceland. The entire country was formed by volcanoes along the Mid-Atlantic Ridge, a chain of mostly underwater mountains. The ridge stretches 10,000 miles (16,093 km) from inside the Arctic Circle nearly to the Antarctic Circle. Along the ridge, lava oozes upward through deep rifts in the ocean floor. The lava spreads outward and builds upward, forming new land where it rises above the ocean. Iceland is the largest part of the Mid-Atlantic Ridge to break the ocean's surface.

Eldfell hurls out lava bombs above the town of Vestmannaeyjar (right). After about three weeks of eruption, Eldfell had created a 700-foot (213-m) cone of ash and lava where only a plain had been before. Vestmannaeyjar is a fishing town. The lava threatened to flow into the harbor and block it. Townspeople used seawater to cool the lava and stop it. They pumped the water on the advancing lava 24 hours a day for nearly 2 months. It worked! Instead of filling the harbor, the lava hardened in place, forming a high wall.

ROBERT S. PATTON, N.G.S. STAFF

Newborn island off the coast of Iceland releases steam (left). Surtsey rose from the sea in 1963, the result of a huge underwater eruption. By 1965, the island measured nearly a mile (1$\frac{1}{2}$ km) wide. It rose above the waves as high as a 55-story building.

H. SIMON/TOM STACK & ASSOCIATES

Most people have never experienced the fury of a volcanic eruption. In Iceland, however, active volcanoes are common. Eruptions can be frightening, and they can cause damage. But volcanoes can also provide benefits—as the people of Iceland have learned.

One important product of volcanic activity is geothermal energy—natural heat, steam, and hot water produced inside the earth. Near volcanoes, magma inside the earth heats underground water. Using pipes and wells, Icelanders draw off the resulting steam and hot water. They use the steam to power electric generators. They use the water to heat buildings. Warming greenhouses, the hot water helps give Icelanders fresh fruit and vegetables the year round. The mighty forces of inner earth may make parts of Iceland rumble and even erupt from time to time. But they also provide geothermal energy—a gift from our violent earth!

Exhaust pipe releases steam at a heating plant on the Eldfell lava flow. Icelanders have found ways of putting volcanic power to work. At Eldfell, the thick lava flow of 1973 has not yet fully cooled. Water piped underground becomes so hot that it boils and turns into steam. Pipes carry the steam to the surface, where it is used to heat houses and other structures. Such naturally heated water and steam are forms of geothermal energy.

SIGURGEIR JÓNASSON

"**C**ome on in; the water's fine!" Bathers in Reykjavík, the capital of Iceland, crowd into a pool filled with volcanically heated water (right). The onlooker at right wears a heavy fur coat to stay warm in the chilly air. An island country, Iceland was formed by volcanic activity on the ocean floor. Iceland is rich in geothermal energy. Nearly all its homes and businesses are heated with steam or hot water piped from under the ground.

N.G.S. PHOTOGRAPHER EMORY KRISTOF

3
STORMY WEATHER

by Robin Darcey Dennis

Spinning across the Dominican Republic, Hurricane David flipped this airplane onto the roof of a hangar as if it were a toy. This 1979 storm thrashed the Dominican Republic with winds estimated at 145 miles (233 km) an hour. Then it pointed its fury at the Florida coast. A hurricane may leave thousands of people homeless. People may be injured, or even killed. One hurricane can destroy billions of dollars' worth of property. Fearsome as they are, hurricanes are just one kind of stormy weather. Another kind of storm, the summer monsoon, is greeted by people in large areas of the world as the "giver of life." It brings the rains that make crops grow.

SISKIND/GAMMA-LIAISON

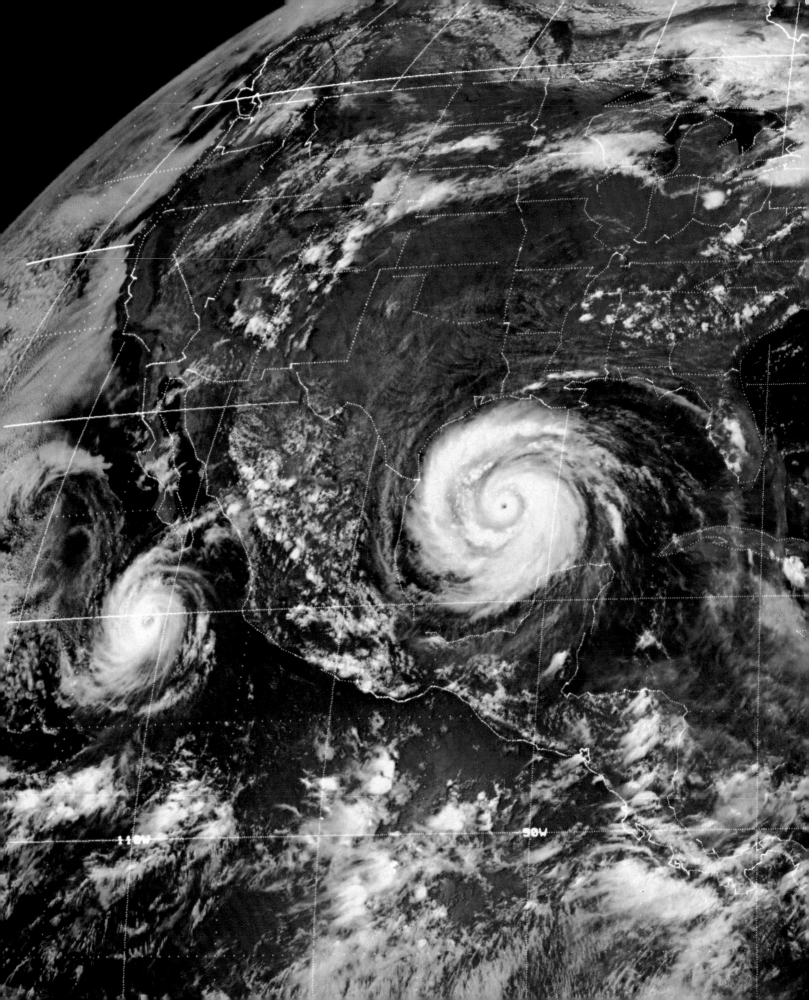

Hurricanes

Every year, the summer sun heats tropical oceans. Above the warm water, whirlwinds form. Most disappear harmlessly. But some combine to form tropical storms — storms with winds of 39 to 73 miles (63–117 km) an hour. If the winds reach 74 miles an hour, such storms officially become hurricanes. They are the biggest, most powerful storms on earth.

Hurricanes don't always hit land. But when they do, they can destroy most things in their paths. Their whirling winds may blow at more than 200 miles (322 km) an hour. Their clouds carry billions of tons of water that has evaporated from the ocean. Hurricanes dump this water on the land in sheets of rain, causing floods. The most dangerous part of a hurricane is the storm surge — a huge bulge of ocean water that sweeps over a coast when a hurricane reaches land. The storm surge is like a giant bulldozer. It can change the shape of the coastline in minutes.

Like giant pinwheels, two hurricanes swirl toward the coasts of Mexico and the United States (left). Satellite pictures such as this one show where storms are forming and where they are heading. The pictures help meteorologists, scientists who study the weather, decide whether a hurricane threatens coastal areas.

NATIONAL EARTH SATELLITE SERVICE/NOAA

Meteorologists at the National Hurricane Center, in Miami, Florida, keep a close watch on Hurricane David (right). Gilbert Clark uses satellite pictures to track its course. Bob Case, on the phone, gives out the latest bulletin. When the hurricane neared land, the meteorologists warned communities in its path.

N.G.S. PHOTOGRAPHER JOSEPH H. BAILEY

Tied securely against the coming winds, pleasure boats in the Florida Keys await Hurricane David (right). Owners moved their boats to these sheltered waters from more exposed areas. The hurricane's powerful winds lashed Florida's Atlantic coast. When people are warned of an approaching hurricane, they can sometimes protect their property against damage, as the owners of these boats did.

N.G.S. PHOTOGRAPHER ROBERT W. MADDEN

Buses take people inland, out of a hurricane's way (left). Evacuating an area—leaving it—is often the safest course for people on the coast. That's where hurricanes hit hardest. The storms can also do serious damage inland before they weaken and die. Officials warn threatened communities so residents can get away safely. When officials advise evacuation, people should leave as quickly as possible.

Preparing for Hurricane David, a worker tapes the windows of a Miami restaurant. Hurricane winds toss heavy objects around easily. Crisscrossed tape sometimes prevents windows from shattering when they are hit by the force of the wind or by flying objects. In the United States, hurricanes cause damage totaling millions of dollars almost every year. The amount of damage keeps increasing, because more and more people are living in areas where hurricanes strike. Now, with better warning systems, fewer people are losing their lives to hurricanes.

N.G.S. PHOTOGRAPHER JAMES P. BLAIR (LEFT AND ABOVE)

45

Fred Werley, a U. S. government pilot, heads his airplane into Hurricane David. "It's risky work," says Werley, "but necessary for getting accurate information about a storm." The hurricane shows on a radarscope to his right.

Sunshine greets Werley's plane as it enters the clear eye, or center, of the storm (below). The plane first had to fly through winds that gusted to 180 miles (290 km) an hour.

Flying Into a Storm's Fury

Few people would fly into a hurricane on purpose. But for some pilots, it's all in a day's work. "Flying into the middle of a hurricane is the best way to gather information on a storm," says Fred Werley, a pilot with the National Oceanic and Atmospheric Administration. Pilots like Werley are called hurricane hunters. Radar—plus piloting skill—helps them pick the safest path through the violent storms.

Hurricane hunters fly to areas where satellite pictures show that hurricanes are forming. Over a period of days, the pilots may fly into a storm several times. Aboard the plane, weather scientists, called meteorologists, measure and track the storm. They send reports to the National Hurricane Center, in Miami, Florida. Meteorologists there use the reports to make forecasts. Other scientists use the information in their search to understand more about—and maybe someday even to tame—the mighty storms.

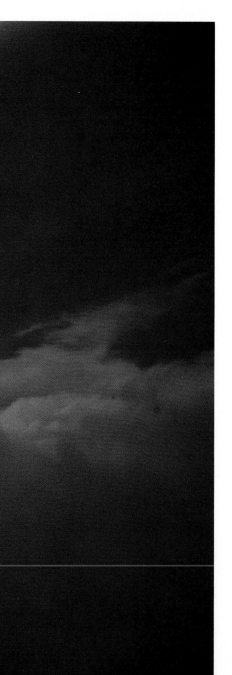

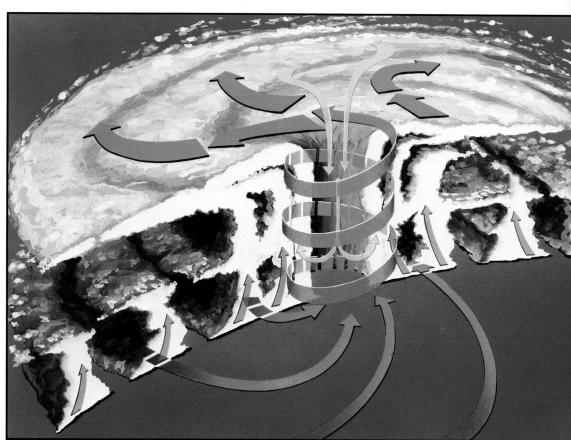

Most hurricanes form in the summer and fall, when the ocean is warmest. In the cutaway view above, warm, moist air rises from the ocean. As the air rises, it cools, forming rain clouds (orange arrows). The earth's rotation starts these clouds spinning into a giant whirlwind that sucks in more warm, moist air. Red arrows show the path of that air. It whirls in an inward and upward spiral. As it rises, it sheds its moisture in sheets of rain. The air spins fastest at the circular wall around the eye of the storm—the eye-wall. Finally it escapes at the top and fans out. Downdrafts pull some of this air—now dry and clear—into the eye (yellow arrows). That is why, in the very center of a raging hurricane, there may be blue sky and sunshine. The eye-wall marks the inner limits of the wind, so the eye may be calm as well as clear.

BARBARA GIBSON

Three pelicans in Corpus Christi, Texas, face the winds of Hurricane Allen in 1980 (below). If the birds don't take cover soon, the storm may sweep them up and carry them hundreds — even thousands — of miles from home.

Pounding a beach in Miami, hurricane wind and rain bend large trees and churn the ocean (right). Hurricanes pack tremendous destructive power. The deadliest hurricane on record in the United States tore into Galveston, Texas, in 1900. Residents of the island city hadn't realized how violent such a storm could be, so only a few had moved inland to safety. Of those who stayed, 6,000 died.

In 1979, high tides and winds of Hurricane Frederic lashed these homes on Dauphin Island, Alabama. Coastal homes such as these are in great danger during a hurricane. Despite the danger, more and more people are building homes on the Atlantic and Gulf coasts. Experts worry that a severe hurricane could destroy huge numbers of homes.

After the Storm

Hurricanes usually die soon after reaching land—but not soon enough to keep them from doing great damage. They sometimes destroy entire communities. They blow down power lines. They wash away roads. After a hurricane strikes, people must clean up the mess it leaves behind.

But hurricanes have some helpful effects. They relieve long dry spells. They stir food up from coastal floors and river bottoms for fish to eat. Most important, they help distribute the sun's heat around the globe. Hurricanes draw evaporated water from over the ocean. The water holds great quantities of excess heat. When the storms move toward cooler climates—as they usually do—they release the heat. Wind and rain result. In this way, hurricanes help moderate, or balance, the earth's climate.

Glad to be alive, Pete Patronas hugs a friend who also made it through Hurricane Frederic (above). On Dauphin Island, 24 people and 2 dogs waited out the frightening storm. Many, like Patronas, were hurt by flying glass or other objects. Some people were rescued from piles of wreckage. All considered themselves lucky to have survived. The storm destroyed almost everything on the island.

HURRICANE FACTS

- If it could be put to use, the energy released by a hurricane in one day would supply electricity to the entire United States for about three years.
- Pacific Ocean hurricanes are called typhoons. Those in the Indian Ocean are called tropical cyclones.
- Since 1900, hurricanes have killed 13,000 people in the United States and caused damage totaling more than 12 billion dollars.
- During World War II, U. S. military meteorologists started naming hurricanes. They named the storms after their wives or sweethearts. Names made it easier to relay information about the storms.

BARBARA GIBSON

At a restaurant in Corpus Christi, workmen remove water left by Hurricane Allen. Years ago, most seaside structures were built on stilts. High waves washed harmlessly under them. Then people began to construct houses and stores without stilts. Though less expensive to put up, such buildings caught the full force of hurricane waves. Now stilts are back in style.

HERMAN J. KOKOJAN/BLACK STAR

Monsoons

In India, people don't cancel festivities because of rain. In fact, the coming of the rainy season is cause for rejoicing. The villagers at this hilltop temple in eastern India are celebrating the festival of Jagannath, lord of the universe. It is a major festival—and it is usually held in pouring rain. These people welcome the drumming of rain on umbrellas. For four months, they have endured the blistering heat of the dry season. Cooling rains mean relief. More important, rains mean more food. Rice—a main part of the Indian diet—grows primarily during the rainy season. This cycle of dry weather followed by drenching rains is the work of shifting winds. The winds, and the seasons they bring, are called monsoons.

BRIAN BRAKE/PHOTO RESEARCHERS, INC. (ALL PHOTOGRAPHS)

Fed by monsoon rains, a river in India overflows its banks. The rains bring needed water to dry areas. The rainy season, or summer monsoon, is a time for planting and tending crops. It's also a time for caution. Flooding rivers often sweep away houses built along the banks.

"Giver of life." That's what many people call the rainy season, or summer monsoon. In many regions, people's lives turn with the cycle of the monsoons. During the winter monsoon, the land dries and hardens. Few crops will grow without irrigation. Food may be scarce. People wait eagerly for the rains to come. Summer will change the earth almost magically. Grass and flowers will spring to life. Fields will sprout with rice.

Along with the rains often comes disaster: floods, landslides, and disease. Every year the rainy season claims thousands of lives in such occurrences. Today several monsoonal countries are building dams and irrigation canals. The governments hope these projects will help prevent such disasters—and provide water for growing crops in the dry season.

Rain in India washes over a woman's face, bringing a smile (above). The summer monsoon and the winter monsoon last about four months each. Between monsoons, the weather is mixed.

Six weeks into the rainy season, rice in a field in India has grown tall and green (right). Soon farmers will harvest it and plant a second crop. In the dry season, the earth bakes hard. Most crops can't grow.

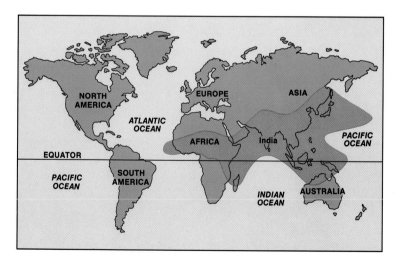

Changing Winds

Monsoons occur in many regions (orange area, left). They result from temperature differences between land and sea. Here's how the process works in India. During the wet season, the sun stays north of the Equator. The sun heats the land more than it does the sea. The hot air over India rises. Cooler, moist air from the Indian Ocean blows in to take its place. The land warms that air, causing it, too, to rise. When air rises, it becomes cooler. The moisture in it condenses, forming the clouds that spill the monsoon rains. During the dry season, the pattern reverses. The sun moves south of the Equator. Now the air over India is cooler than air over the sea. The warmer sea air rises. Air from India blows out to take its place. In turn, dry air from farther inland sweeps over India.

GARY M. JOHNSON, N.G.S./ADAPTED FROM MONSOON METEOROLOGY, BY C.S. RAMAGE © 1971, ACADEMIC PRESS, INC.

55

Lightning

Lightning and thunder are familiar partners in a thunderstorm. The sharp clap of thunder may sound scary, but it's the lightning that packs the punch. In an instant, one of these bright bolts of electricity can splinter a tree, damage a house, or start a forest fire. Lightning kills more people in the United States every year than hurricanes or tornadoes do.

Thunderclouds are storehouses of electrical energy. The lower part of a cloud carries negative charges; the top part carries positive charges. The earth beneath a thundercloud also builds up positive charges. The opposite charges attract each other like magnets. But air between the two charges insulates them—it keeps them apart. When a cloud builds up enough electricity, however, the opposite charges overcome the insulation. A flow of electricity—lightning—results. As the lightning flashes, it heats the air in its path. The air expands with a loud crash—thunder!

Some lightning travels harmlessly within clouds or between them. But when lightning streaks to earth, it can be dangerous. On the poster in the back of this book, you'll find tips for keeping safe in thunderstorms.

During a storm, lightning scored a hole in one on this Arizona golf course (above). The lightning struck the flagpole, then burned the grass as it streaked along the ground. Lightning usually strikes the tallest object around on its way to the earth. That's why you should never stand under a lone tree or in an open space during a thunderstorm.

E. P. KRIDER/UNIVERSITY OF ARIZONA

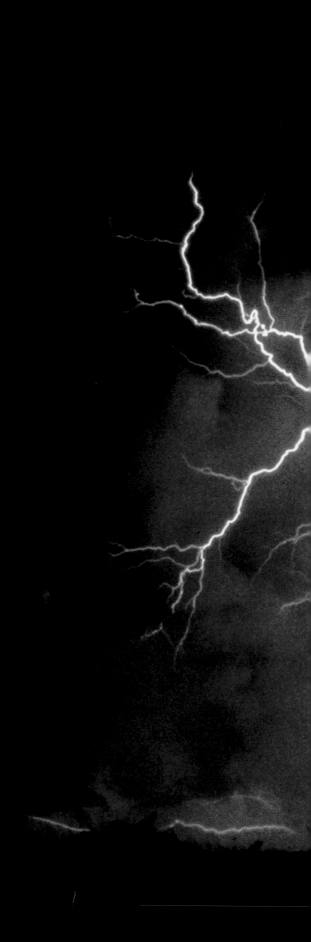

Nature's fireworks light up the sky during a thunderstorm over Harbour Island, Bahamas. Lightning flashes when clouds release huge amounts of electrical energy. A single bolt may strike the earth with 100 million volts of electricity. The lightning may be hotter than the surface of the sun.

BARRY PARKER/BRUCE COLEMAN INC.

Tornadoes

Roaring like a freight train, a tornado whips out of the cloud-blackened sky. It spins across the land, tracing an unpredictable zigzag path. It pulls trees out of the ground. It rips the roofs off houses and sends them sailing across the sky. It picks up cars and trucks and drops them hundreds of yards away.

The winds of such a tornado are the fastest on earth. They can whirl at a speed of 250 miles (402 km) an hour. Luckily, most tornadoes are not so violent. They have weaker winds, and they travel only short distances. Most tornadoes occur in the countryside, where few people live. But when even a small tornado whirls through a community where many people live or work, it can cause heavy damage in just a few minutes.

Whirling toward a farmhouse, a tornado fills the sky (large picture). Like most tornadoes, this one took a crooked path as it spun over prairie land near Wichita, Kansas. It swung away, missing the farmhouse.

Tornado left a Texas family with a sense of humor, at least. In The Wizard of Oz, a tornado whirls Dorothy's house to the Land of Oz. In reality, tornadoes often rip houses into splinters.

Tornadoes strike in the United States more often than they do in any other part of the world. About 700 tornadoes, or twisters, are reported in the United States every year.

Meteorologists haven't yet discovered exactly why tornadoes form. They do know that the twisters are most likely to occur in the spring. That's when warm, moist air moves up from the south and collides with cooler air from the north. The collision of different kinds of air often causes violent thunderstorms. It is out of such thunderstorms that tornadoes are born. A tube of swirling winds—the funnel—descends from the thunderclouds. It sweeps and bobs along the ground, shattering objects in its path.

The National Weather Service uses radar, satellites, and computers to help predict when and where tornadoes will occur. Engineers study the damage tornadoes do to buildings. They are learning how to design buildings that will stand against a tornado's frightening power.

Twisters Small and Large

Tornadoes come in many shapes and sizes. Some are tall and narrow, others short and wide. The paintings below show three common shapes of tornadoes. 1. Most small tornadoes have a funnel that looks like a snake twisting down from the clouds. Sometimes such tornadoes form over water; then they are called waterspouts. 2. The funnels of many medium-size tornadoes are narrow near the bottom; they widen toward the top. 3. The biggest tornadoes often look like a dark cloud wall. The clouds are so dark and so close to the ground that the funnel may be barely visible.

BARBARA GIBSON

Tornado drill has these Kentucky schoolchildren up against a wall. They are practicing taking cover in a safe place. If a real tornado comes, these third graders will know what to do. The National Weather Service warns people about tornadoes. When the Weather Service announces a tornado watch, *it means the weather is right for a tornado.* When it announces a tornado warning, *it means a tornado has been spotted.* It's time to take shelter, as these youngsters are doing.

JAY MATHER

SAFETY TIPS

- If you live where tornadoes often strike, stay alert for weather bulletins.
- Plan what you will do if a tornado strikes. Remember, a tornado warning means "Take shelter!"
- At home, go to the basement or to the lowest level of your house. Crouch under the stairs, under sturdy furniture, or along an inside wall. Cover your head with your hands.
- In a public building, go to a storm shelter if there is one. If not, go to an inside hallway on the lowest floor. Crouch down and cover your head.
- If you're outside and don't have time to find shelter, lie flat in the nearest ditch or other low area.

BARBARA GIBSON

Scattered wreckage littered this neighborhood in Louisville, Kentucky, after a tornado struck in 1974 (near right). The tornado threw pieces of houses and trees everywhere. The storm followed a zigzag path. A tornado often flattens one house and leaves the one next door untouched. The picture at far right shows the same neighborhood only seven months later. Residents rebuilt the neighborhood, leaving little sign of the tornado's destruction.

© 1974, THE LOUISVILLE COURIER-JOURNAL, BY C. THOMAS HARDIN (BOTH)

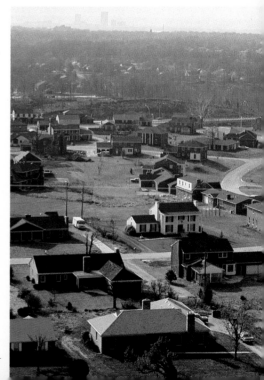

Blizzards

This may happen to you some winter morning. You rise at your regular hour to get ready for school. As you brush your teeth, you glance out the bathroom window and see—snow! A thick white blanket covers everything. Overnight, a blizzard has struck. Schools, offices, and stores are closed. No one can travel the snow-covered roads.

A blizzard is a storm that brings heavy snow to an area. It can start suddenly and be over in a few hours. Some blizzards last for days. Wind can pile the snow to rooftop level. The heavy snow may bring everything to a halt. Until the snow melts or work crews move it out of the way, people can't get to stores, offices, hospitals—anywhere.

During a blizzard, fiercely cold winds blow and the temperature drops below freezing. "This kind of weather can fool you," says Don Witten, of the National Weather Service. "The thermometer might say 30°F [–1°C]. But when the wind is blowing, the temperature outdoors feels much lower than 30°." Wind can chill you faster than you think. "During a blizzard," says Witten, "the wisest thing to do is to stay indoors."

Blinding snow almost hides youngsters stepping off a school bus at their farm home near Worthington, Minnesota. Wind, cold, and blowing snow make a dangerous combination. In bad blizzards, people trying to reach home have lost their way just a few feet from their own front doors.

JIM BRANDENBURG

Forecast: Snow!

In some places, such as Canada and the northern United States, people expect blizzards during the winter. They keep extra food and other supplies on hand. If a snowstorm cuts them off from the rest of the world, they easily survive. But when people aren't ready for a blizzard, food and fuel may run short. With roads blocked, many people can't leave their homes. Thousands of people might need food, fuel, or medicine. At such a time, rescue workers are called on to deliver emergency supplies.

Usually, weather forecasters can warn a community a few days before a blizzard strikes. They keep track of cold-air masses that are moving across the country. Now forecasters are improving their ability to make long-range predictions, as well. In the fall of 1976, they forecast an unusually cold, snowy winter. The prediction proved accurate. For the first time on record, every state except Hawaii had snow on the ground at the same time. The map below shows how air currents miles above the earth's surface can bring on such bitter weather.

JET STREAM

ARCTIC FLOW

SUBTROPICAL FLOW

Much of the weather in North America is brought by the jet stream. That's a current of strong, chill winds that circle the globe about 8 miles (13 km) above the surface. Two lower altitude currents—the arctic flow and the subtropical flow—also carry weather with them. In the winter, the jet stream normally takes the path shown on the map above. The stream carries moist Pacific air to the western states. Sometimes, however, it moves off course. That changes the weather. In the winter of 1976–77, for example, a section of the jet stream moved far north, to Alaska. The stream poured arctic air into the eastern states. It dodged the western states altogether. The result? The eastern states shivered, and the western half of the country suffered drought.

VJ 9925

SAFETY TIPS

- Keep ahead of the weather. Listen to weather bulletins.

- Stay indoors during storms and very cold periods. Keep a supply of food on hand. Have an emergency source of heat and a battery-powered radio.

- If you must travel by car, make sure the fuel tank is full. Try to travel with other cars, in a convoy. Carry blankets, matches, and a food supply in the trunk.

- Outdoors, wear loose clothing in layers. The outer layer should be of water-repellent material. Inner layers of wool will keep you warmest.

After a blizzard, these residents of Wilmette, Illinois, break out their skis for a trip to the store (above). Cars and buses are useless when a thick blanket of snow covers roads. After a heavy blizzard, many people may be snowed in. Rescue workers must bring in supplies. The workers get through any way they can—on skis or on snowshoes, in helicopters or in snowmobiles.

FAVERTY/GAMMA–LIAISON

School days are cold days for these youngsters in Toledo, Ohio (left). They wear their winter coats in class because their school has run out of heating fuel. In the unusually cold winter of 1976–77, furnaces ran overtime to keep buildings warm. Before long, many areas ran out of fuel. Ships carrying fuel were locked in ice as the Ohio and Mississippi Rivers froze over, adding to the problem.

HERRAL LONG

4
DROUGHT AND FIRE

by Robin Darcey Dennis

"A wall of dust thousands of feet high was coming toward us. When it hit, the sky was as dark as night." That's how one witness described a dust storm in Marrakech, Morocco (right). It swept through the North African city in 1975. When strong winds blow across dry earth, they sometimes stir up dust storms. If the topsoil is loose and powdery, the winds pick it up and whisk it away. Such storms sweep across the land, sometimes carrying with them hundreds of tons of rich topsoil. Dust storms are just one of the troublesome effects of drought (say DROWT). A drought is a long period of dry weather. Not enough rain falls to keep plants and animals—and sometimes even people—alive.

JOHN ELK III/BRUCE COLEMAN INC.

Crops suffer when the land dries up. Texas farmer Ferris Sherman (right) holds an ear of corn withered by drought. During a drought, the land suffers, too. Normally, moisture and the roots of grass, trees, and crops hold the rich topsoil in place. When dry weather kills off plant life, wind rakes the bare topsoil away, sometimes turning a region into a wasteland. Years may pass before such land becomes fertile again.

68

Thirsty Land

Heat from the sun causes ocean water to evaporate. The water vapor forms into clouds, and the water returns to the earth as rain. Around the world, different places receive different amounts of rain each year. When a region gets much less rain than normal, it usually suffers a drought.

A drought may not be recognized until the damage has begun. At first, people may be glad to see clear, sunny skies. But when the clear weather goes on too long, it can mean disaster. Without rain, grass and crops wither and die. Farmers have nothing to feed their livestock. Dry winds blow the soil into clouds of dust. The water supply shrinks.

In the United States, drought usually hits one region or another and has little effect on the country as a whole. In the drought-stricken regions, however, the dryness destroys the land. Farmers are hit the hardest. Many are forced out of business when a drought continues for years.

In some countries, if crops and livestock die for lack of water, the people may have nothing to eat. They may have no food reserves and no money to buy food from abroad. When that happens, other countries often donate food. Sometimes, however, the relief is too little or it comes too late. As a result, people may starve.

But people can fight drought. Long ago, farmers learned that they couldn't always depend on rain to water their crops. If they wanted to grow

Severe drought in 1977 left Lake Shasta, California's largest reservoir, 142 feet (43 m) below its normal level. The tree line along the shore shows how high the lake usually is. Normal demand drained so much water from the lake that the boathouse, at left, had to be moved hundreds of feet. Otherwise, some boats might have been left high and dry.

LOWELL GEORGIA

Dried and cracked, this land (right) was once a riverbed. Then drought came, and the river dried up. The land is in a region of Africa called the Sahel. It stretches along the southern edge of the Sahara. Here people search for water-lily bulbs to eat. Drought came to the Sahel in 1968. Crops died. Grazing animals stripped the land of grass, which could not grow back without water. The drought lasted five years. As a result of the drought, 250,000 people and millions of animals died.

GEORG GERSTER

enough food, they had to irrigate the land—bring water to it. Some farmers call irrigation "rented rain." Rain is free, but building and maintaining an irrigation system can cost millions of dollars.

For centuries, people have used canals to carry water from rivers and lakes to their crops. Irrigation canals that may have been built 4,000 years ago still carry water to Egyptian fields. If a drought lasts long enough, however, even the rivers and lakes dry up. In some areas, pools or rivers of water lie underground. People can dig wells and use the underground reservoirs to meet their water needs.

Some crops grow even in deserts. In Israel, a desert country, farmers raise crops by recycling the little rain that falls. They have built huge greenhouses that trap moisture and send it trickling back into collection tanks. They have laid underground pipes that give just the right amount of water directly to plants at their roots, wasting nothing. Such projects take hard work and a lot of money. But the effort pays off. Israel, which once had to import most of its food, now helps feed other nations of the world.

Building a greenhouse, workers in the Negev dig trenches for pipes to heat the ground. Heated ground makes crops grow faster. Pipes are also used for "trickle irrigation." Water seeps through holes in the pipes, wetting only plant roots. That way, water is not lost through evaporation or by soaking into the ground.

Recycling rain makes a little go a long way. In the Negev, greenhouses keep water from evaporating into the outside air. Vapor condenses, or turns to water, on the plastic walls inside. As a woman picks green peppers (below), water runs down the wall. It will be collected and used again. Israel hopes someday to have thousands of acres covered by huge plastic bubbles. Inside such desert domes, the climate could be controlled to produce the largest harvests possible.

NATHAN BENN

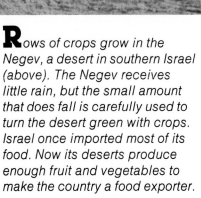

Rows of crops grow in the Negev, a desert in southern Israel (above). The Negev receives little rain, but the small amount that does fall is carefully used to turn the desert green with crops. Israel once imported most of its food. Now its deserts produce enough fruit and vegetables to make the country a food exporter.

TOR EIGELAND (ABOVE AND RIGHT TOP)

Land Ablaze

More than half the United States is covered by forests and grasslands. All too often, these areas become fuel for raging fires. In dry summer months, the tiniest spark can set timber blazing in minutes. Sometimes forest fires burn for many days. Trees and other vegetation burn to the ground. As forest fires spread, they may reach areas where people live. Then homes go up in flames.

People are to blame for most forest fires. Only one fire out of ten starts naturally, usually when lightning strikes a tree. People start the other nine—mostly through carelessness.

A major fire might bring 2,000 fire fighters from many states. They come armed with various equipment and skills. Computer experts calculate the fire's likely path. Pilots look for trouble areas. Fire brigades use bulldozers and shovels to clear a strip of ground. The strip, called a fire line, will help keep the fire from spreading. Specially equipped airplanes are used to drench the blaze with water and chemicals. Fire fighters called smoke jumpers parachute into areas unreachable by road.

When fires rage out of control, they are violent destroyers. But with modern equipment and methods, fire fighters today are saving more woodland than ever before.

*B*one-tired and blackened with soot, a smoke jumper leans on his shovel (left). Smoke jumpers parachute into hard-to-reach areas to battle forest fires. Here a blaze started by lightning burns in Suislaw National Forest, in Oregon.

DAVID FALCONER

*F*ighting fire with fire helps control a blaze in Oregon's Winema National Forest. Fire fighter Ed Heilman lights a backfire (right). It will burn out grass between the fire and the fire line—a strip of bare ground cleared to stop the advance of the flames. "It's a lot safer to set a controlled backfire than to let the big blaze work its way to the fire line," says Heilman. "This way, the blaze has less chance of jumping across the fire line." Before this fire was brought under control, it destroyed 15 square miles (39 sq km) of forest.

CHRISTOPHER JOHNS

Fires aren't always a cause for alarm. Tribesmen in Tanzania, a country in eastern Africa, purposely set fires like the one below to burn off dead grass. New, green grass will soon grow in its place. It will feed the tribe's cattle. Grass fires attract many insect-eating birds. Here a kori bustard waits to make a meal of insects trying to escape the blaze.

Its tips burned by fire a month earlier, a saw palmetto still grows green and healthy (left). In the Florida pine woods where palmettos live, fires are common during long dry spells. Plants like this one have adapted to fire —they survive and grow after a blaze. Some trees survive because they have very thick bark that is almost fireproof. Certain kinds of pine trees even need fire. They can't release their seeds until the heat of a fire makes their cones burst open.

SAFETY TIPS

- Use matches only with adult supervision. Make sure used matches are cold before throwing them away.

- Never leave a campfire untended. When putting out a campfire, drench it thoroughly, until it stops smoking. Then stir up the ashes, double-checking for any live coals.

- If your clothing catches fire, remember this rule: stop, drop, roll. That will put out the flames. Running will only fan them.

- At home, post the fire department number by each telephone. Learn how to report a fire quickly and clearly.

A SPECIAL STORY
CALIFORNIA: FIRE AND RAIN
by James A. Cox

Smoke rises from burning brush on hills around Mandeville Canyon, near Los Angeles. When the flames finally die, the stage will be set for another problem. There's a saying in southern California: "Flood follows fire."

JOHN BRYSON/SYGMA

Spark Hazard. *As a wall of flames advances over the hills, a resident of Mandeville Canyon wets down the roof of a house. The roof is made of wood shingles. Wind-driven sparks could easily ignite the roof if it were left unprotected. In this area, dry summers and miles of brushland combine to make fire a yearly threat.*

Destructive Cycle

California has two serious problems that work hand in hand to cause destruction. One is fire. The other is flood. Both problems are more serious in the southern half of the state, where many people live in areas troubled by frequent fire and flooding. During summer, millions of acres of forest and brushland become as dry as straw. Every year, thousands of fires start. In just one month in 1970, southern California suffered through 1,260 forest fires and brush fires. They burned thousands of acres, destroyed hundreds of buildings, and killed 14 people.

Fire fighters put out most blazes. But some fires cannot be controlled. Fanned by hot, dry winds, they race over hillsides covered with brush and grass. When the flames finally die out, the slopes are nearly bare. Most of the plant life is gone. And so is much of the network of roots that helped hold the soil in place.

Winter brings rain. Water flows down the bare hills, causing erosion—the wearing away of the soil. Topsoil washes into rivers and reservoirs, turning the water a muddy brown. Floods sweep down on valley communities. Some water soaks into the hillsides, making the soil heavier. In time, the extra weight causes the earth to slide. Masses of mud flow down the slopes, carrying rocks and brush. Mud slides block roads. Sometimes the land slides out from under (Continued on page 82)

Mud Slide. *After heavy rains, homeowners in Glendora fight a river of mud, brush, gravel, and boulders. Most residents were able to dig out and clean up. But some lost the battle. Mud slides destroyed 5 homes and damaged 160 others.*

N.G.S. PHOTOGRAPHER BRUCE DALE

Fighters. *Battling roaring flames in Los Padres National Forest near Big Sur (left), fire fighters use flares to set a backfire. They hope the backfire will burn toward the big blaze, depriving it of fuel.*

After the Fire.

Kimberly Adams, 12, of Malibu, examines her ruined bike (left). Flames burned the tires right off the wheels. The fire started in Malibu on October 23, 1978. "We had a Santa Ana wind condition—a big, hot wind," recalls Kimberly's father, Gary. "The fire raced across the 10 miles [16 km] to the ocean in less than 2 hours. It wiped out nearly everything in its path." The Adamses lost their home, but saved their pets: 3 horses, 2 goats, and 9 rabbits. The family later built a new house on the same hilltop, but this time chose fireproof tiles instead of wooden shingles for their roof.

CRAIG AURNESS/WEST LIGHT

Treeless Forest.

A cloud of smoke, and hills covered with ashes and rocks —that's about all that remained after fire swept through Los Padres National Forest (right). It was 1977, and California was experiencing a severe drought. People hoped the dryness would not lead to fires. But the fires came. They burned an area more than half the size of Rhode Island. They killed 16 people and destroyed 700 homes. Then came the rains, the heaviest in years. Mud flowed down the treeless hillsides, flooding entire communities. Such flooding sometimes causes worse damage than the fires do.

© CAROL BERNSON, 1977 (OPPOSITE AND RIGHT)

79

Rushing Water. *Citizens of Glendora stack sandbags to battle floodwaters. They hope to direct the flow to an area where there are no houses. Their efforts—and their joking sign—failed. Seconds after this picture was made, a mighty rush of water swept away the barricade and headed for their homes.*

Big Job. *Weary worker takes a break from digging out after the Glendora flood (right). To avoid a repeat of this 1969 disaster, the city is improving its dams and its system of storm drains.*

Roadblock.

Landslide blocks the eastbound lanes of the Pomona Freeway (below), normally a busy highway in the Los Angeles area. Now heavy equipment digs in to carry away the mass of earth. Rains soaked through the bare surface of this slope. The water lubricated a layer of clay, causing layers of earth above it to slide. Engineers say that cutting stair-step patterns, called terraces, into such slopes will help prevent future slides.

J. R. EYERMAN

Sliding Hillside.

"I always wanted a sunken living room," says Sharon Geltner with a bitter laugh. A rain-soaked hillside slid out from under her home and swimming pool in Encino (below). Mrs. Geltner and her husband, Peter, saved their furniture with the help of 20 friends and several vans. But nothing could save the $200,000 house. "We can't repair it," Mrs. Geltner says. "There's no ground left to repair it on."

N.G.S. PHOTOGRAPHER JODI COBB

(Continued from page 77)   a house, sending it crashing downhill.

An earthquake can trigger landslides, too. The 1971 San Fernando quake set off more than a thousand rock falls. Most lasted from a few seconds to a few minutes. But not all slides are over so quickly. Landslides may occur very gradually. Hillsides—and the houses on them—slip inches a day for months at a time.

Landslides also happen in other parts of the United States. They threaten areas of Washington State and Oregon. The Rocky Mountains in the West have them, as do the Appalachians in the East.

Scientists are studying the causes of landslides. They hope to identify places where landslides are most likely to occur. Then people can avoid building homes in those areas. In California, laws now regulate construction in areas troubled by floods and landslides. New housing developments have to be provided with good storm-drain systems to control the runoff of rainwater and mud. New fire-prevention and weather-forecasting methods also are helping to reduce the toll in lives and property. But despite the regulations and scientific advances, fire and rain still spell big trouble for southern Californians.

New Look. *Floods and mud slides present a challenge to builders in southern California. To protect a section of Hollywood called Mount Olympus —the flat-topped area below—developers cut terraces into steep slopes and dug storm drains. Older homes perched on other hillsides, left, do not have such protection. They were put up before Los Angeles toughened its building regulations.*

N.G.S. PHOTOGRAPHER BRUCE DALE

5
WATER

by James A. Cox

Pedestrians in Venice, Italy, use a temporary walkway to cross floodwaters. Floods like this one, which occurred in 1971, endanger this city of 150 canals. Venice was founded about 1,500 years ago by Italians fleeing invaders from the north. The founders built the city on a group of islands near the coast in the northern Adriatic Sea. The islands have been sinking into the sea for many years. High tides often cause floods. Buildings in the city rest on wooden posts that the water is slowly wearing away. To make matters worse, the dikes built to protect Venice are being washed away, and Venetians haven't agreed on a way to rebuild them. Water once protected Venice from its enemies. Now water threatens the city's survival.

ALBERT MOLDVAY

Floods

On November 4, 1966, the people of Florence, Italy, awoke to find the narrow streets of their city filled with swirling water. For two days, unusually heavy rains had fallen on northern Italy. The rains swelled the Arno River, which flows through the heart of Florence. The rising river finally spilled over its banks. In one square, the water was 23 feet (7 m) deep. The disaster killed 17 people in Florence. Thousands had to leave their homes. Muddy water damaged two million priceless rare books and more than a thousand of the art treasures that make Florence famous.

Floods like the one that struck Florence occur in many parts of the world. Usually flooding results from a long period of heavy rain. But a quick downpour sometimes causes rivers to *(Continued on page 90)*

Floodwaters from the Arno River swirl through an intersection in Florence, Italy (left). People trapped in the building on the right get a closeup view of the scene. This 1966 disaster damaged or destroyed many of the city's famous art treasures.

HOLLY LAPRATT

Mud-smeared volunteer rescues a book from the flooded basement of the National Library (above). Throughout the city, the flood damaged two million treasured books.

ELIO SORCI

Bookbinders worked with student volunteers from many countries to save thousands of volumes. Here soggy pages are hung out to dry in the furnace room of the Florence railroad station.

BALTHAZAR KORAB

FLOOD FACTS

- The most destructive flood in recorded history occurred in China in 1887. The Hwang Ho (Yellow River) spilled over its banks, killing 900,000 people.

- In the United States, flooding is the most widespread geological hazard. Half the nation's communities regularly face floods.

- Much of Holland lies below sea level. The Dutch have built dikes to hold back the North Sea. Without the dikes, high tides would flood the lowlands.

BARBARA GIBSON

Over millions of years, the Little Colorado River, in Arizona, has been cutting a canyon, below, left, deep into desert rock. The river does its work during only three months of the year. For the other nine months, the river is usually dry. Here a Navajo Indian on the far bank watches the river take a 130-foot (40-m) plunge at Grand Falls.
GEORGE H. BILLINGSLEY

Sculptor at Work

Waterfalls act as natural chisels. Falls like the one pictured below often form where river water wears through a layer of hard rock to expose soft rock underneath. The water erodes, or wears away, the soft rock faster than it does the hard rock that remains. In time, the edge of the hard rock becomes the top of a cliff over which the river spills. The water gnaws at the soft rock underneath, and pieces of the cliff break off. In this way, a waterfall slowly moves upstream. Geologists say Niagara Falls has worked its way upriver nearly 7 miles (11 km) since it was formed about 12,000 years ago.

BARBARA GIBSON

HARD ROCK

SOFT ROCK

Shaped by the action of water, Devils Tower juts 865 feet (264 m) from rolling hills outside Sundance, Wyoming (left). The tower is the core of an ancient volcano. Over millions of years, water wore away the outer layer —the cone. Raindrops, acting somewhat like tiny bombs, splattered away much of the cone, particle by particle. Streams eroded the rest. This hard core will eventually be washed away, too. Some Indians believed an evil spirit lived in the peak. In their language they called the formation "The Bad God's Tower." The Army colonel who mapped the area in 1875 translated the name as "Devils Tower."

N.G.S. PHOTOGRAPHER DEAN CONGER

89

(Continued from page 87) spill over their banks without warning. Such floods are called flash floods. In some areas, floods come regularly with spring weather. Rising temperatures melt winter snow, sending meltwater into rivers. It swells them until they overflow.

During floods, rivers spill onto adjoining flat areas called floodplains. People who live on floodplains can sometimes protect themselves by building dikes along the riverbanks to hold back rising waters. They can also build dams upriver to hold water and control its flow. Architects can design buildings that keep floodwaters out.

Although communities built on floodplains must often deal with the ill effects of floods, they may also benefit from the fertile soil that flooding provides. In Egypt, for example, flooding of the Nile River deposits layers of rich silt on the land. This yearly process makes the Nile valley one of the most fertile regions in the world.

Iowa River overflows its banks near East Amana, Iowa (above). The river floods every two to five years. Worldwide, floods take more lives and destroy more property than any other kind of natural disaster. But floodwaters often have a helpful effect. They deposit layers of mineral-rich earth on croplands.

N.G.S. PHOTOGRAPHER STEVEN L. RAYMER

Concrete slabs reinforced with steel cables help keep a riverbank from eroding. The bank lies along a section of the Mississippi River, near Reserve, Louisiana. Engineers lay such slabs on the outer banks of river bends, where erosion is most severe. By preventing the banks from being washed away, the slabs help control flooding. Slabs like this one line portions of the Mississippi River from Cairo, Illinois, to the river's mouth below New Orleans, Louisiana.

N.G.S. PHOTOGRAPHER JAMES L. STANFIELD

Glaciers

Glaciers are huge bodies of ice. They form in very cold places, such as high mountain valleys, where snow piles up. The snow turns to ice. Over hundreds of years, the ice mass becomes bigger and heavier. Pulled by gravity, it starts to move down a valley. Most glaciers travel no more than 2 feet (61 cm) a day. But some, moving in spurts, have advanced 150 feet (46 m) in a day.

Geologists believe that glaciers have sculpted much of the earth's surface. During the Ice Ages of the past two or three million years, glaciers covered roughly the northern half of North America. They gouged out lake beds and built hills. Today glaciers hold about three-fourths of all the fresh water in the world. Scientists are working on ways to use glacial ice. Someday ships may tow icebergs, which break off from glaciers, to desert areas. There the icebergs would provide fresh water for drinking and for growing crops. Scientists are also trying to find ways to control the flow of glacial meltwater so it can be used to run power plants.

Twenty miles (32 km) from Juneau, Alaska, Taku Glacier mows down a section of pine forest (above). Scientists walking on the leading edge measure the glacier's advance. Glaciers like Taku have shaped many parts of the earth's surface.

Deep cracks, called crevasses, surround geologists studying the movement of Taku Glacier (right). Crevasses (say crih-VASS-iz) form when one part of a glacier moves faster than other parts. In one year, Taku advances nearly 500 feet (152 m).

Geologists in Canada measure the depth of the Columbia Icefield (right). In places, the ice is as deep as the Empire State Building is tall! Ice fields are huge sheets of ice. Often they are the birthplace of glaciers. As an ice field thickens, dozens—even hundreds—of glaciers may start to flow from it. Gravity causes the movement. It pulls glaciers downhill along the valleys they occupy.

Lakes Born of Ice

Geologists believe that at least four times in the past—during the Ice Ages—glaciers covered the five river valleys that now hold the Great Lakes (below). Each time the glaciers advanced, they gouged the valleys even deeper than before. The last Ice Age reached its peak about 20,000 years ago. By 14,000 years ago, the glaciers were melting and retreating. The river valleys filled with water. Land that had been pressed down by the weight of the ice gradually rose back. The rising land dammed existing outlets, holding the water in its basins. By 10,500 years ago, the vast pools had taken on much of the familiar shape of the Great Lakes today. Fed by the melting glaciers, the rising water found an outlet to the northeast. The water flowed through that outlet, creating the St. Lawrence River.

WILLIAM H. BOND, N.G.S.

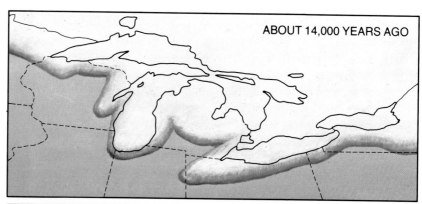

ABOUT 14,000 YEARS AGO

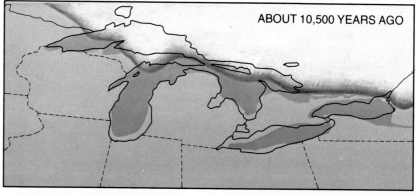

ABOUT 10,500 YEARS AGO

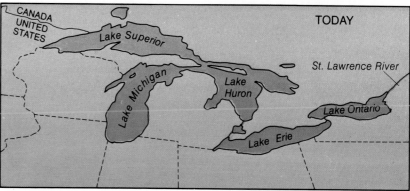

CANADA
UNITED STATES

TODAY

Lake Superior

Lake Michigan

Lake Huron

St. Lawrence River

Lake Ontario

Lake Erie

River of ice, the Athabasca Glacier (above) pushes through the Canadian Rockies. The glacier has crept out from the Columbia Icefield. Ice melts at the tip of the glacier. The meltwater has a milky color, which comes from rock that the glacier has ground into powder. Every day, the glacier dumps into a nearby lake a mass of powder weighing more than a fully loaded jumbo jet. Water from the Columbia Icefield runs into three oceans: the Pacific, the Atlantic, and the Arctic.

Avalanches

Whoosh. No crash, crack, snap, or boom announces the start of an avalanche, or snowslide. Often, the only warning is a soft, shuffling sound. A moment later that sound has grown to a roar as masses of snow rip down a slope. Most avalanches travel at 50 to 200 miles (80–322 km) an hour. The fastest avalanche on record was clocked at 280 miles (451 km) an hour —faster than the top speed of most racing cars. An avalanche may last only minutes, but its power is enormous. It can wreck a house or derail a train in the wink of an eye.

The formula for an avalanche is simple: a lot of snow plus a steep slope. Many things can trigger an avalanche. The weight of a skier can start one, as can the slicing action of skis. Vibration can start one. So can changes in temperature. Sometimes temperature changes cause the snowpack to freeze hard, then melt slightly, then freeze again. At certain points in such a cycle, parts of the snowpack may weaken. Acting in combination or separately, all these things determine *(Continued on page 99)*

Ski patroller at Snowbird Ski Resort, in Utah, hurls a hand charge into a snowdrift (above). In the early morning, before skiing begins, Snowbird patrollers scout the slopes for dangerous snowdrifts. When they find one, they throw or fire an explosive into it. The resulting explosion triggers a snowslide. That way, an unexpected avalanche probably won't occur later.

Exploding hand charge, thrown from a helicopter, starts tons of snow tumbling down a slope in Utah. The first chunk of snow to break away was as big as a railroad boxcar As it streaked downhill, it shook loose more snow. Avalanches sometimes travel with racing-car speed. They can create winds of hurricane force.

97

An avalanche tossed cars around like toys in this hotel parking lot in Alta, Utah. It flung a pickup truck into a second-story hotel room! The tumbling snow buried most of the 13 other vehicles on the lot. This avalanche occurred in 1980. A ski patroller set off the slide deliberately—but it was bigger than expected. It started in a large natural bowl where miners in the 1800s had cut down most of the trees. A wall of snow $4^1/_2$ feet ($1^1/_2$ m) high and 300 feet (91 m) wide broke loose. With few trees to slow it, the avalanche roared over the parking lot at 100 miles (161 km) an hour.

SAFETY TIPS

- In steep, snowy areas, hike or ski with a companion. Cross dangerous slopes one at a time. If one of you is caught in an avalanche, the other can provide help.

- If your boots or skis cause long cracks in the snow, you're on dangerous snow. Turn back!

- Run or ski away from an avalanche. If you can't escape, try to grab on to a tree or a bush. If that fails, take off your skis and your backpack. Make swimming motions with your arms and legs. That will help keep you at the surface.

Liam Fitzgerald, director of snow safety at Snowbird, takes samples of snow at the fracture line where an avalanche started (left). Comparing these samples with samples taken from snowdrifts in the area will give him clues to where other avalanches are likely to occur.

Squinting through a magnifier, Fitzgerald examines the structure of snow grains (above). Scientists recognize more than 100 types. Some, shaped like stars, stick together well. Others, shaped like balls, may not stick together at all. Star-shaped snow is less likely to start sliding.

(Continued from page 96) whether snow will stay on a mountainside or come thundering down.

In the 1940s, scientists in the United States began to study avalanche control. The studies took place in the vicinity of Alta, Utah. A popular ski center, the region averages 40 feet (12 m) of snow a year. It has more avalanches than any other populated area of North America.

Avalanche hunters at Alta have learned a lot. They know where to expect avalanches. They study the snow in those areas, looking for lines of weakness where a slide is most likely to start. "It takes a well-trained eye to see these lines," says John Loomis, assistant mountain manager of Snowbird Ski Resort. "There are layers in snow, much like the layers in a cake. Sometimes the layer that starts a snowpack tumbling is hardly thicker than a pencil."

Avalanche workers can prevent an uncontrolled slide about 70 percent of the time. Trained ski patrollers go out at dawn after every snowstorm to check the slopes. Some ride in helicopters. Others travel over trails on skis. When they see snow that appears likely to slide, they start it moving with explosives. Then, when several hundred skiers hit the slopes later, there are no deadly *whoosh*es.

Preparing to battle dangerous snowdrifts, a Snowbird ski patroller carries explosive shells to the surface from an underground storage room (above). Empty storage casings lie along the sides of this tunnel floor. The storage room itself is made of steel and concrete. It is located a safe distance from the ski area. The patroller will fire the shells from a small cannon called a recoilless rifle, a weapon once commonly used in warfare.

Before going out on the trail, Snowbird ski patroller Nan Rogers assembles explosive shells (left). She will fire these shells from a weapon called an avalauncher. The avalauncher was invented in 1962 especially for the control of avalanches. It has a range of about one mile (1¹⁄₂ km).

Bursting from a cloud of smoke, an explosive charge from a recoilless rifle speeds toward a dangerously swollen snowdrift (right). You can see the shell on the left side of the smoke cloud. The large flash at right is caused by gases escaping from the weapon. Ski patrollers set the gun on a platform near the top of a peak and aim it at known trouble spots. Although they are now largely out of date as military weapons, recoilless rifles are still valuable in avalanche control.

Thinking Ahead: Careers in Earth Sciences

How can we harness the power of a lightning bolt? Are there ways to predict earthquakes with pinpoint accuracy? What's the best way to prevent Venice, Italy, from disappearing into the sea?

Right now, no one is sure of the answers to these questions. But many people have chosen careers in which they try to find the answers. **Geologists,** for example, study the structure of our planet. Some geologists look for new sources of geothermal energy. Geologists who work with oil companies use their knowledge to find promising places to drill for petroleum and natural gas. Others seek new beds of coal and deposits of minerals. Some geologists do research and teach.

Miles above us, a complex system of air currents helps bring about the constantly changing weather we experience on earth. **Meteorologists** study earth's weather. Some meteorologists predict seasonal and day-to-day weather. Their forecasts help farmers plan the best time for planting and for harvesting. Their warnings of violent storms help save lives. Other meteorologists do research. They seek to improve our understanding of weather behavior and climate changes.

Oceans cover most of the earth's surface. Scientists called **oceanographers** study the oceans. They trace ocean currents and map the ocean floors. Some oceanographers search the seabeds for deposits of vital minerals and fuels.

You don't have to be an earth scientist to work with the forces of nature. Many people choose work that allows them to help victims of natural disasters. **Communications technicians** and **public-health experts**, for example, work with the Red Cross and other relief agencies. When a flood, fire, earthquake, or some other disaster strikes, they rush to the scene to aid the injured and the homeless. Sometimes people with unusual skills volunteer their knowledge to repair the damage caused by a natural disaster. During the 1966 flood in Florence, Italy, bookbinders were among the heroes. They helped save a part of the city's treasure.

Some people work to prevent injury or damage that might result from natural disasters. **Forest rangers** keep an eye out for fires. When a fire starts, **fire fighters** jump into action to save lives and property. In some snowy areas, **ski patrollers** scout the slopes, looking for skiers in distress. Sometimes patrollers also help in avalanche control. **Engineers** build dams and other structures that help control floods. **Architects** design buildings that resist floods and earthquakes.

One day you may decide on a career in one of these fields. The work can be exciting, whether it takes place outdoors or in. You might choose to be a **helicopter pilot** who goes on rescue missions. Or you may work as a **laboratory researcher** who makes important discoveries about the earth's makeup.

You can find more information about careers such as these in your school or public library. A librarian will be happy to help you find books on the subject. Your guidance counselor can also give you career information.

Index

Composition for OUR VIOLENT EARTH by National Geographic's Photographic Services, Carl M.
Shrader, *Chief;* Lawrence F. Ludwig, *Assistant Chief.* Printed and bound by Holladay-Tyler Printing
Corp., Rockville, Md. Color separations by the Lanman-Progressive Corp., Washington, D. C.; and
Lincoln Graphics, Inc., Cherry Hill, N. J.

Library of Congress CIP Data
Main entry under title:
Our violent earth.
(Books for world explorers)
Bibliography: p.
Includes index.
SUMMARY: Describes the causes and effects of such geologic and atmospheric phenomena
as earthquakes, volcanoes, storms, drought, fire, and flood. Includes a wall poster, games, and
puzzles.
1. Natural disasters—Juvenile literature. [1. Natural disasters. 2. Earth sciences] I. National
Geographic Society (U. S.) II. Series.
GV5019.087   363.3'4   80-8797
ISBN 0-87044-383-6 (regular binding)   AACR2
ISBN 0-87044-388-7 (library binding)

Robert W. Decker, U. S. Geological Survey/Hawaiian Volcano Observatory; J. Murray Mitchell, National Oceanic and Atmospheric Administration; Peter B. Stifel, University of Maryland — *Chief Consultants*

Glenn O. Blough, LL.D., University of Maryland; Patricia Leadbetter King, National Cathedral School — *Educational Consultants*

Nicholas J. Long, Ph. D. — *Consulting Psychologist*

The Special Publications and School Services Division is grateful to the individuals, organizations, and agencies named or quoted within the text and the individuals cited here for their generous assistance:

Michael E. Bickford, Weyerhaeuser Co.; David Blankenship, National Audubon Society; Jim Campbell, National Weather Service; Gilbert Clark, National Hurricane Center; Duane Cooley, National Weather Service; Dick Friend, Los Angeles County Fire Department; T. Theodore Fujita, University of Chicago; Carolyn Habbersett, National Weather Service; John B. Hatcher, U. S. Forest Service; Judith M. Hobart; Robin T. Holcomb, U. S. Geological Survey; Mary F. Hughes, National Oceanic and Atmospheric Administration.

Walter S. Judd, University of Florida; Edwin Kessler, National Severe Storms Laboratory; Jack Krajewski, Schoellkopf Geological Museum; Herbert Lieb; Max Lowdermilk, Agency for International Development; Mike McDermott, U. S. Department of Energy; Maynard M. Miller, University of Idaho; William G. Munro, U. S. Forest Service; Richard E. Orville, State University of New York at Albany; Gudmundur Pálmason, National Energy Authority (Reykjavík, Iceland).

Waverly J. Person, U. S. Geological Survey; C. S. Ramage, University of Hawaii; Thelma Rodriguez, U. S. Geological Survey; Eric Saul, Presidio Army Museum; John M. Stratton, Snowbird Ski Resort; Bill Temple, Los Angeles County Flood Control; Sigurdur Thórarinsson, Science Institute (Reykjavík, Iceland); Marshall Turner, Bureau of the Census; Robert E. Wallace and Jean Whitcomb, U. S. Geological Survey; J. Tuzo Wilson, Ontario Science Centre.

ADDITIONAL READING

Readers may want to check the National Geographic Index *in a school or public library for related articles and to refer to the following books. ("A" indicates a book for readers at the adult level.)*

General: Brown, Walter, *Catastrophes,* Addison-Wesley, 1979. Johnson, Thomas P., *When Nature Runs Wild,* Creative Education Press, 1968. Millard, Reed, *Careers in the Earth Sciences,* Julian Messner, 1975. National Geographic Society, *Our Continent,* 1976 (A). National Geographic Society, *Powers of Nature,* 1978 (A). Navarra, John Gabriel, *Nature Strikes Back,* Natural History Press, 1971.

Earthquakes: Asimov, Isaac, *How Did We Find Out About Earthquakes?,* Walker, 1978. Cazeau, Charles J., *Earthquakes,* Follett, 1975. Fodor, R. V., *Earth in Motion: The Concept of Plate Tectonics,* Morrow, 1978. Matthews, William H. III, *Introducing the Earth,* Dodd, Mead, 1972. Navarra, John Gabriel, *Earthquake,* Doubleday, 1980. Nixon, Hershell H., and Joan L. Nixon, *Earthquakes,* Dodd, Mead, 1981. Weiss, Malcolm E., *Lands Adrift: The Story of Continental Drift,* Parent's Magazine Press, 1975.

Volcanoes: Matthews, William H. III, *The Story of Volcanoes and Earthquakes,* Harvey House, 1969. Nixon, Hershell H., and Joan L. Nixon, *Volcanoes: Nature's Fireworks,* Dodd, Mead, 1978. Poynter, Margaret, *Volcanoes: The Fiery Mountains,* Julian Messner, 1980. Radlauer, Ruth Shaw, *Volcanoes,* Children's Press, 1981. U. S. Geological Survey, *Atlas of Volcanic Phenomena,* U. S. Geological Survey, 1971 (A).

Stormy Weather: Alth, Max, and Charlotte Alth, *Disastrous Hurricanes and Tornadoes,* Franklin Watts, 1981. Aylesworth, Thomas G., *Storm Alert: Understanding Weather Disasters,* Julian Messner, 1980. Berger, Melvin, *The New Air Book,* Crowell, 1974. Bova, Ben, *Man Changes the Weather,* Addison-Wesley, 1973. Buehr, Walter, *Storm Warning: The Story of Hurricanes and Tornadoes,* Morrow, 1972. Cohen, Daniel, *What's Happening to Our Weather?,* M. Evans, 1979. Gallant, Roy A., *Earth's Changing Climate,* Four Winds Press, 1979. Uman, Martin A., *Understanding Lightning,* Bek Technical Publications, 1971 (A). Wachter, Heinz, *Meteorology: Forecasting the Weather,* Franklin Watts, 1973. Weiss, Malcolm E., *Storms — From The Inside Out,* Julian Messner, 1974. *(For more information about the weather, write to* NOAA, *Office of Public Affairs, Rockwall Building, 11400 Rockville Pike, Rockville, Md. 20852.)*

Drought and Fire: Hurst, Randle M., *The Smokejumpers,* Caxton Printers, 1966. Milne, Lorus J., and Margery Milne, *The Phoenix Forest,* Atheneum, 1968. Pringle, Laurence, *Natural Fire: Its Ecology in Forests,* Morrow, 1979. *(See also listings under "Stormy Weather.")*

Water: Fodor, R. V., *Angry Waters: Floods and Their Control,* Dodd, Mead, 1980. Kirk, Ruth, *Snow,* William Morrow & Co., 1978 (A). Lavine, Sigmund A., and Mort Casey, *Water Since the World Began,* Dodd, Mead, 1965. Nixon, Hershell H., and Joan L. Nixon, *Glaciers: Nature's Frozen Rivers,* Dodd, Mead, 1980.

PUBLISHED BY
THE NATIONAL GEOGRAPHIC SOCIETY
WASHINGTON, D. C.

Gilbert M. Grosvenor, *President*
Melvin M. Payne, *Chairman of the Board*
Owen R. Anderson, *Executive Vice President*
Robert L. Breeden, *Vice President,
Publications and Educational Media*

PREPARED BY THE SPECIAL PUBLICATIONS
AND SCHOOL SERVICES DIVISION

Donald J. Crump, *Director*
Philip B. Silcott, *Associate Director*
William L. Allen, William R. Gray, *Assistant Directors*

STAFF FOR BOOKS FOR WORLD EXPLORERS
Ralph Gray, *Editor*
Pat Robbins, *Managing Editor*
Ursula Perrin Vosseler, *Art Director*

STAFF FOR *OUR VIOLENT EARTH*
Ross Bankson, *Managing Editor*
James A. Cox, Robin Darcey Dennis,
Catherine O'Neill, *Writers*
Dennis Dimick, *Picture Editor*
Lynette Ruschak, *Designer*
Mary B. Campbell, Carolinda Hill, *Researchers*
John D. Garst, Jr., Margaret Deane Gray — *Map Research*

FAR-OUT FUN! AND SUPPLEMENTARY ACTIVITIES
Patricia N. Holland, *Project Editor;* Pat Robbins, *Text Editor;* Lynette Ruschak, *Designer;* Barbara Gibson, *Artist;* Peter J. Balch, Art Iddings, Gary M. Johnson, *Mechanicals*

ENGRAVING, PRINTING, AND PRODUCT MANUFACTURE
Robert W. Messer, *Manager;* George V. White, *Production Manager;* Gregory Storer, *Production Project Manager;* Mark R. Dunlevy, Richard A. McClure, Raja D. Murshed, Christine A. Roberts, David V. Showers, *Assistant Production Managers;* Katherine H. Donohue, *Production Staff Assistant*

STAFF ASSISTANTS: Mary Elizabeth Davis, *Editorial Assistant;* Artemis S. Lampathakis, *Illustrations Assistant;* Mary Jane Gore, *Art Secretary;* Nancy F. Berry, Pamela A. Black, Nettie Burke, Jane H. Buxton, Claire M. Doig, Rosamund Garner, Victoria D. Garrett, Jane R. Halpin, Nancy J. Harvey, Joan Hurst, Virginia A. McCoy, Merrick P. Murdock, Cleo Petroff, Victoria I. Piscopo, Tammy Presley, Carol A. Rocheleau, Katheryn M. Slocum, Jenny Takacs

MARKET RESEARCH: Joe Fowler, Marjorie E. Hofman, Carrla L. Holmes, Meg McElligott, Stephen F. Moss, Susan D. Snell

INDEX: Anne K. McCain